APR 2 1 2022

Chinwe Esimai

Brilliance Beyond Borders

Remarkable Women Leaders Share the Power of Immigrace

HARPER HORIZON

This book is dedicated to my family.

Among the greatest gifts in my life are the family with whom I've been blessed to embark on this *ijeoma* (beautiful journey). My husband, Ifeanyi, my children, Tobe, Ola, and Nnamdi— I love you so much. Thank you for your love and support.

My parents, Philomena and Fabian, who gave me the greatest foundation any human could ask for, and my extraordinary siblings: Gozie, Obi, Okey, and KC.

Published by Harper Horizon, an imprint of HarperCollins Focus LLC.

Any internet addresses, phone numbers, or company or product information printed in this book are offered as a resource and are not intended in any way to be or to imply an endorsement by Harper Horizon, nor does Harper Horizon vouch for the existence, content, or services of these sites, phone numbers, companies, or products beyond the life of this book.

Brilliance Beyond Borders and Tap Into Your Immigrace are registered trademarks of Immigrace by Chinwe LLC. All rights reserved.

Brilliance Blueprint graphic by Ni-Ka Ford.

ISBN 978-0-7852-4169-0 (eBook)
ISBN 978-0-7852-4168-3 (HC)

Library of Congress Control Number: 2021939410

Printed in the United States of America
22 23 24 25 26 LSC 10 9 8 7 6 5 4 3 2 1

Contents

Foreword

Brilliance Beyond Borders is an amazing tool to empower immigrant women from diverse backgrounds and provide them the space and instruments to realize their full potential, and to become successful and powerful women leaders, not only in the United States but globally.

In telling the stories of women who have been able to unleash their potential and overcome various types of adversity and build resilience, this book provides an actionable way for all women to obtain the inspiration and motivation to accomplish their dreams. No matter where you're from, if you've been able to cross the bridge, pass through the frontier, and arrive in a place where better opportunities exist, everything is available on the menu for you. The possibilities are limitless.

I believe that Chinwe is a wonderful example. She is not only amazing because of her own story, of which she is a heroine, going through all the barriers and doing her best, and ultimately becoming powerful, but because she is an inspiration for others. Through her level of generosity in reaching out to women, especially immigrant women living in the United States, she is able to create this movement of women who can serve in wisdom.

Brilliance Beyond Borders is a beautiful gift for immigrant women. I believe that no matter where you are right now on your journey, this book reminds you that everyone has a start—sometimes a very rough start—but they still arrive at the destination. So I am very excited to recommend this book because I believe we should not leave anyone without the power of believing!

—BISILA BOKOKO,
Spanish-born American businesswoman of
African descent, entrepreneur, speaker, philanthropist,
United Nations World Citizen Award Honoree, and one of
the 10 Most Influential Spanish Women in American business

Introduction

What if . . . a Jamaica-born, four-time Olympic gold medal–winning champion never stepped foot in the Olympic tryouts?

What if . . . a Vietnam-born, Emmy award–winning film producer and physician never produced a single film?

What if . . . a Russia-born, career architect and genetic researcher who was part of the Human Genome Project and documentary scriptwriter for *National Geographic* never set about the work of unlocking human potential?

What if each of these women never pursued their dreams, but instead remained in roles that represented shadows of their truest potential?

What if the traditional narrative about immigrant success is a lie? According to the story, immigrants who come to the United States will succeed as long as they work hard, stay focused, and have supportive families. The same story also proclaims that a single definition of success is paramount and that the accumulation of degrees and professional success are enough.

If you are living your ultimate dream, the ultimate dream for which you migrated to the United States, and the ultimate dream for which you came into this world, then our work is done.

If, however, you hold bigger, bolder, and more brilliant dreams, but never give life to those dreams, then we, as a society and as humanity, have failed. We have lost out. We have lost out on world-class athletic excellence, breakthrough genetic research that cures diseases, award-winning films that heal and uplift, and infinite possibilities of innovative contributions to our communities and our world.

And the American Dream will continue to be a lie for millions of immigrant women here in the United States.

Of the approximately 69 million women in the US workforce as of 2020, 10.4 million are foreign-born.[1] The truth is, even in the midst of headlines and political debates about immigration reform and since the rise of the MeToo movement, millions of immigrants, especially women, are not living up to their potential.

You may recognize some of these conditions because you may have lived or are living one or more of them:

- You have a college or graduate degree, but are deep in student loan debt, carry various forms of debt, and fear that you may never be financially free.

- You are broke, working multiple jobs to make ends meet, pay the bills, and support your family, while scraping together a few hundred dollars to send to family members in your home country.

- You are taking ill-advised steps to fit into American society. You may have changed your name from Jinghua to Lucy, from Udoka to Jane, or from Alejandra to Sandra.

- You are working incredibly hard every day. In spite of your hard work, best intentions, and resilience, you're unhappy, living as a shadow of your truest potential, and feel like a ship at sea, without a clearly defined destination.

- You are uncertain about how to honor your history while creating a brighter future for yourself and your family.

If any of these feels familiar, you are not alone. But you'll never realize your fullest potential if you buy into the lie.

As an antidote, we'll explore the indispensable traits that make an ocean of difference between immigrants who live as mere shadows of their truest potential and those who build incredible, world-changing legacies.

We'll ask a much better "What if" question. What if all immigrant women leaders embraced their genius, lived their purpose, and created mind-blowing legacies?

Stories are powerful to uncover truths, make common the so-called uncommon truths and "secrets," combat isolation, shatter myths, and serve as guides on our chosen paths.

Breaking Our Silence

Sue* never spoke up during my securities regulation class. She was one of two women in a class of fifteen law students in a course I taught while I was a law professor. The men spoke often—they were confident and talkative, even when they hadn't read the materials.

One day after class, Sue came up to me with a question. She was almost apologetic for interrupting my exit, and her voice was so soft I had to incline my head to hear her. It was the best question I'd heard all semester, and I wished she had asked it during the class. It would have been a teachable moment to drive home some key points.

A bit puzzled (although in retrospect, I should not have been), I asked her why she didn't ask her question before. She smiled, lowering her eyes and staring at her boots. She was too nervous to speak to the whole class, she said. She went on to clarify that she'd come to the United States from Korea for law school and hadn't been in the country for very long. She was acutely conscious of her foreign accent.

---

* Student has been anonymized.

I explained to her that I knew exactly how she felt. When I was a freshman at the City College of New York and a seventeen-year-old immigrant from Nigeria, I was just like her: shy, reserved, and too nervous to express my views. I told her I remembered those days—the feeling that everyone sounded more knowledgeable than me because they didn't have foreign accents.

Sue's eyes widened as she leaned closer toward me. "You, Professor?" To her, the professor who marched across the classroom, seemingly very comfortable in her own skin, was a far cry from a nervous immigrant.

With some encouragement, by the end of the semester Sue shared her views in class.

What Sue didn't realize was that in asking her question that day, she taught me that every immigrant woman has a story to tell. As I searched for resources to support Sue on her journey, I was surprised to discover that there were none focused entirely on immigrant women as leaders. There was, however, an abundance of social science research on immigrant women, most of them heavily academic that evaluated our demographics and factors such as refugee status, rape, and other forms of domestic violence.

The Quest for Role Models

After leaving academia, I had similar experiences of outreach from young professional immigrant women seeking mentors. While pregnant with my third child and working at Goldman Sachs, almost on a weekly basis, acquaintances directed their friends and relatives to me. These included: high school students who aspired to attend Harvard or other Ivy League institutions; college students on their way to law school; and women embarking on journeys to corporate America or recently returning to work after having children, with work/life balance on their minds.

My acquaintances had a simple ask: speak to them about your experiences or mentor them, if you have time. I quickly realized that there were three common denominators among all the individuals who were referred to me: they were women, immigrants, and had a burning desire to excel.

I began to do some more research on key attributes of successful immigrant women leaders, both by speaking with immigrant women and reading. I get passionately curious about topics that fascinate me, and the study of immigrant women is one such topic. After speaking to thousands of women around the world, mentoring professional women across the United States, and engaging with readers of my blog and listeners to my podcast, here is what I found:

- Women are underrepresented in nearly all professions, particularly at the highest levels. For example, I was surprised to learn (as discussed in chapter 1) that women composers represented only 16 percent of works featured in contemporary orchestral concerts and performances. Over the last few decades, as women have entered academic institutions and the workplace, there has been a growing need for resources to accompany them on their journeys from entry-level to mid-level and the most senior-level roles.

- Immigrant women feel like double outsiders—as women in male-dominated fields, and as individuals born and raised in countries other than the United States who are navigating a new culture that in certain respects may conflict with the cultures in our home countries.

- While a number of women's leadership books have entered the market and assisted women to navigate professional life, none has done so from the perspective of immigrant women, therefore leaving the second outsider angle unattended.

- As immigrant women, we are eager for relatable life and leadership stories, and want to hear from those who have walked in our shoes. We have questions about how to authentically assimilate, how to thrive through difference, how to speak up and stand out, and how to do these things without forgetting who we are and where we came from.

Returning to the high-achieving immigrant women that were referred to me, I spoke to them and offered myself as a resource, but I also wanted to help provide sustainable and enduring empowerment. I didn't want to *tell* them how I did it, I wanted to *show* them how, and encourage them on an ongoing basis.

Perhaps most importantly, I did not want them to hear from me alone. I had encountered many phenomenal immigrant women throughout my education and career, and I knew there were others they could look to as examples that their dreams are infinitely possible.

That is how this book was born.

Women in the Workplace and the Pandemic Paradox

As I write this, women in the workforce face a paradox. The paradox is that while women in professional roles have grown and made great strides over the last several decades, the pandemic has significantly slowed down or reversed much of that progress. In 2021, for example, Jane Fraser took her seat as the first female chief executive officer in Citigroup's over-two-hundred-year history. Kamala Harris serves as the first female vice president in over 244 years of United States history. Indra Nooyi, currently on the board of directors of Amazon, completed a successful tenure as chief executive officer of PepsiCo from 2006 to 2008 and served as PepsiCo's chair of the board till 2019.

Yet the coronavirus pandemic has thrown the workforce into unprecedented chaos. With job losses, companies and entire industries going out of business, and the prevalence of remote work, what were historically conceived as workday hours stretch well beyond their traditional scope and space. Concurrent with their workday commitments, and in addition to typical homework obligations, working mothers now juggle homeschooling responsibilities.

While the worldwide impact of the pandemic has been evident, the *Wall Street Journal* 2020 Women in the Workplace Report took a closer look to analyze its impact on professional women. It noted that many women, especially mothers, had to step back or away from jobs because of the pandemic's impact on their careers. According to the report, which surveyed more than forty thousand North American employees, while women represent 47 percent of the US labor force, they accounted for 54 percent of initial coronavirus-related job losses and still make up 49 percent of them. The report also found significant impacts on women with children, senior women (with responsibilities for teams), and Black women. As one who falls into all three categories, I can personally attest to the emotional toll and challenges of the past year.

In a full-page *New York Times* ad, Girls Who Code founder Reshma Saujani, leading a group of fifty prominent women leaders (including Dee Poku Spalding, profiled in this book), called upon President Biden to implement a Marshall Plan for Moms. According to the National Women's Law Center, more than two million women have left the US workforce since the pandemic began in 2020. A December 2020 report from the Bureau of Labor Statistics noted that women were leaving the workforce at four times the rate of men.

Employers and governmental leaders have struggled to address these pandemic challenges, and the threat is that the gains made over decades of female representation in the workplace have been eroded in a matter of months.

In the midst of the challenges presented by the pandemic, we are at a point of opportunity. The opportunity is to redefine the aspects of the old models in the workplace that have become untenable. The rigid and structured models will give way to the definition and re-evaluation of hybrid and flexible models that support performance and well-being. This book hopes to stand for freedom, and for the passion, promise, hope, and inspiration of women leaders as we navigate today's complex, challenging, and beautiful world. The women of *Brilliance Beyond Borders* are warriors, having been shaped by some of the greatest political struggles, conflicts, and upheavals of the twentieth century and indeed, human history, including: the Vietnam War, Cambodian Genocide, Nigerian Civil War, Iranian Revolution, Philippines People Power Revolution, Chinese Cultural Revolution, and the Soviet Union.

This book celebrates the values that draw immigrants to the United States and unite us as Americans. It hopes to be a companion and guide to set and reset standards of brilliance at home, at work, and in your life.

My middle name, Ijeoma, means "beautiful journey" in Igbo, my Nigerian language. Journeys fascinate me because they suggest progress, growth, change, discovery, anticipation, and adventure. We usually have expectations about what we will find on our journeys, but there is also the possibility that we may yet discover something new and unexpected.

I hope that you will not only learn from and be uplifted by the stories and contributions of the extraordinary women profiled here, but that you, regardless of where you are in the world, and whether you are a first-, second-, or fifth-generation American, will embrace the Brilliance Blueprint; serve the world around you with heart, faith, and brilliance; and build your own remarkable legacy.

How This Book Is Structured

We explore the indispensable traits that make an ocean of difference between immigrants that live as mere shadows of their truest potential and those that build incredible, world-changing, and mind-blowing legacies. Each section includes the Brilliance Blueprint, a step-by-step guide to enable you to build your own remarkable legacy.

To illustrate the exceptional contributions of immigrant women in American society and, more importantly, the wide array and infinite possibilities available to immigrant women, the book includes the stories of seventeen trailblazing women from all continents around the world and several industries, including sports, music, medicine, fashion, broadcasting, and law. The Brilliance Blueprint, which summarizes the key themes in each section, is your guide to creating your own extraordinary life.

- Each section begins with an introduction, which outlines the primary theme in the section.

- It is then followed by three or four chapters of women's stories.

- We begin each chapter with a brief biography, then explore each woman's immigrant journey, key turning points in her life and career, her definition of success, and wisdom and advice for other women (we call these bits of guidance *immigems*).

Think of immigems as the gemstones that make up the Taj Mahal, one of the new seven wonders of the world, designated by the United Nations Educational, Scientific and Cultural Organization (UNESCO) as a World Heritage site.

The Taj Mahal consists of brick and white marble from Agra, jaspers from Punjab, jade and crystal from China, turquoise from Tibet, sapphire from Sri Lanka, and carnelian and lapis lazuli from Arabia.[1] Use these immigems, along with the stories of the women from all around the world, to build you up—your personal edifice and your own wonder of the world. Your Taj Mahal.

- We also identify each woman's immigrant genius (we call it *immigrace*, described in more detail in part I).

- Each section concludes with the Brilliance Blueprint theme and an Immigrace Journal which guides you in applying the lessons to your life. For me, it was important to incorporate the Brilliance Blueprint and Immigrace Journal to enable you to write your own story. There's a temptation, especially for women, when we read about others' successes, to think that it is not possible for us. My quest is to annihilate such temptation and support you in demonstrating to yourself that it is possible to realize the life you were born to live.

In *The Road Less Stupid: Advice from the Chairman of the Board*, Keith Cunningham said: "Having the right answer is smart. Having the right question is genius." I'm a firm believer in the power of questions and have experienced massive breakthroughs and transformations in my life by asking the right questions.

The answers are all within you; the Immigrace Journal reminds you how brilliant you are. Through the power of questions you can access the truth and knowing within you. You don't need to limit yourself to the questions in the Immigrace Journal. Think of them as prompts, but you can come up with your own transformational and hopefully, more impactful questions. One of the greatest skills we can develop is the ability to ask ourselves disruptive questions, and as difficult as it may be, to pinpoint our own disempowering stories and blind spots.

The Brilliance Blueprint consists of five steps. Each step is described in more detail in each of the respective sections. While the steps are outlined in logical order, they are mutually reinforcing and form part of an ongoing and never-ending immigrace journey.

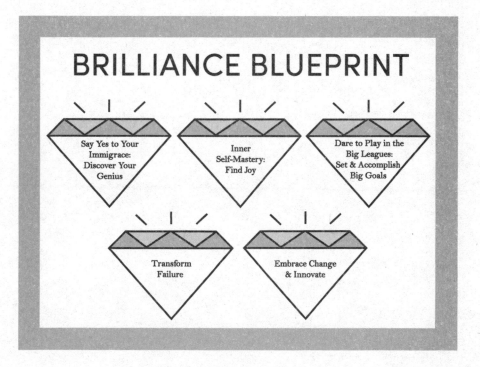

BRILLIANCE BLUEPRINT

Say Yes to Your Immigrace: Discover Your Genius

Inner Self-Mastery: Find Joy

Dare to Play in the Big Leagues: Set & Accomplish Big Goals

Transform Failure

Embrace Change & Innovate

PART I
Say Yes to Your Immigrace
Discover Your Genius

How many life-altering truths do you figure we reject or ignore on a daily basis? In my opinion, there are at least thousands of radical, world-changing realities around us that could make a profound difference in our lives that we routinely reject or ignore.

Take, for example, the definition of *genius*:

> ***genius*** • ˈjēn-yəs | ˈjē-nē-əs
> a strong leaning or inclination • a peculiar, distinctive, or identifying character or spirit • the associations and traditions of a place • a personification or embodiment especially of a quality or condition • a single strongly marked capacity or aptitude • extraordinary intellectual power especially as manifested in creative activity • a person endowed with extraordinary mental superiority especially: a person with a very high IQ • showing or suggesting great cleverness, skill, or originality: brilliant[1]

You may have noticed, as I have, that somehow, as a society, we disregard the various definitions of *genius* and limit ourselves to "a person with a very high IQ." It's fascinating how limited we are in discussing such a powerful and expansive word. Not brilliant at all, and not of optimal benefit to us individually and collectively.

The truth is that *genius* does have a variety of forms and manifestations, and *genius* also represents, not only our "endowed" gifts and inborn inclinations, but also the gifts that we can and should develop over time.

Each of us, at various points in our lives, have exhibited, touched, or lived our genius, whether by displaying a strong leaning or inclination, reflecting a peculiar distinctive or identifying character or spirit, demonstrating the associations or traditions of a place, personifying or embodying a special quality or condition, demonstrating a single strong marked capacity, demonstrating extraordinary intellectual power in a creative activity, or showing or suggesting great skill, originality, or, my personal favorite, brilliance.

Yet most of us also reject or resist the idea that we are all geniuses. As though Einstein, Michelangelo, Picasso, and Isaac Newton are cut from different cloth, born with special, untouchable, unapproachable gifts, we place them on finely carved, engraved, and embossed pedestals. It is also noteworthy that the individuals typically associated with genius tend to be mostly men. A personal dream, and thank you for sharing in it by reading this book, is that references to genius do not lead us to default to images of men, like Einstein, but that we recognize and acknowledge the genius of women. More than sixty years after Einstein walked the earth, it's time to upgrade our genius software. It's time to evolve our visual and mental representations of genius, including by recognizing and acknowledging those he's inspired over the years and those who have come after him.

On a short list of eleven female geniuses, Fairygodboss.com—a career community for women—includes Sau Lan Wu, born in Hong Kong and immigrant to the United States. She played a major role in the discovery of the Higgs boson in particle physics theory. Marie

Curie, Polish immigrant to France and pioneering physicist and chemist, who won Nobel prizes for her work on radioactivity, occasionally makes an appearance in discussions of genius.

We must change the traditional misconceptions about genius because we know they are fundamentally flawed. We know that each and every day, women contribute in extraordinary ways to the growth, evolution, and significant improvements in our world.

It is also a lie because we are all born with special gifts within us. The problem is, as we journey through life, we hide, cover up, lose, erode, reject, or forget those gifts, due to life experiences, disappointments, and our focusing on life's most pressing and immediate priorities. Worse still, based on experiences, we develop beliefs that contradict this fundamental truth.

Once upon a time, education was designed for the purpose of uncovering individuals' gifts, talents, and even genius. Today we know it so often falls short of this lofty aim. It is not unusual to encounter people who have decades of education and very little idea what sparks their interest or how they can uniquely contribute to the world.

Some resist the idea that we are all geniuses and they warn that we would somehow diminish the power of the word, on the premise that "if everyone is a genius, no one is a genius." Rather than seeking to maintain the exclusivity of the word, how about we focus on elevating people, so that we collectively elevate our life experiences through the power of creativity, passion, and of people living their fullest potential? I'm not for the trivialization of genius, but for the democratization of genius. To make it understandable, discernable, approachable, accessible, and available to all, should they choose to embrace it and attain that high level of greatness we are all capable of.

I advocate for demystifying concepts, principles, and ideas. Once demystified and available to all, I don't believe demystification automatically leads to irreverence. We can know and understand something or someone, yet still respect, revere, and treat them as sacred. This is the stuff that extraordinary marriages and relationships are made of. In fact, in my experience, when something or someone is truly beautiful and brilliant at their core, the more you know them, the more you love, appreciate, respect, and revere them.

Like a beautiful marriage that creates enormous joy within those in and around it, my quest is to help you fall in love with your genius, value it enough to make time and space for it, nurture it and grow it, so that through it, you create joy within yourself, those around you, your community, and our world.

This brings us to the definition of immigrace. Let us now examine the definition of *immigrace*:

immigrace • ʹimēgrās/ | ʹiməgrās
immigrant's grace • immigrant's genius • unique gifts each
immigrant woman brings into the world • an immigrant's
expression of her highest purpose and potential

Immigrace is immigrant's grace and, more to it, immigrant's genius. *Immigrace* stands for the unique gifts each immigrant woman brings into the world, and into the United States. It is an immigrant's expression of her highest purpose and potential.

All human beings come into this world with unique gifts and talents, but for us as immigrant women, regardless of what age we migrated to the United States, we carried within us big, bold dreams and the highest expression of our life's purpose. The United States, as the greatest freedom experiment in the history of mankind, stood for the incubator in which all of our highest dreams could be created, honed, and launched into the world.

Immigrace and Being

Less than specific goals and accomplishments, immigrace is first and foremost about who we are in the world. It's about the presence we bring to our work and how we choose to live.

I advocate for the preeminence of being. Even the experts on the subject of genius, of whom I've gained tremendous insights over the years, tend to speak of genius as something you do, a place you visit, or a place in which you operate. Robert Greene explores the attainment of mastery—something you get. He studies masters such as Einstein and Freddie Roach and talks about primal curiosity, learning above all else, gathering skills, and combining skills in a unique way. *The Big Leap* by Gay Hendricks is also a wonderful exploration of the idea of genius, and speaks of functioning in your genius zone, which Hendricks brilliantly distinguishes from the zone of incompetence, the zone of competence, and even the zone of excellence. But in my estimation, there's a sense in which it is a place you go and that it could be outside of you. Robin Sharma's *The 5AM Club* expounds on how the practice of rising early enables people to take control of their day. That said, I think they would all agree that who we are is preeminent.

I also argue for the preeminence of who we are because the joy is unquestionably in the journey. The radical beauty and learnings in life are not embedded in our loftiest intentions and goals, but they unfold and become evident in who we become in the process. We explore joy in more detail in Part II.

With that in mind, let's consider the core characteristics of immigrace.

Core Characteristics of Immigrace

- *Natural Inclination:* Immigrace is rooted in and honors the natural gifts, inclinations, and interests of the individual. Immigrace is not only one thing and can relate to multiple gifts, interests, and purposes. As we evolve and our journeys evolve, our purposes do as well. As we increase in strength, we set new goals and destinations.

- *Eternal:* Immigrace is not time-bound, but includes a commitment to growth, continuous experimentation, and ongoing learning. It seeks to touch on something beyond this world, ditches perfection, and embraces the journey, uncertainty, and not having all the answers.

- *Purposeful and Legacy-Driven:* Immigrace is a commitment to living the purpose for which we were placed on earth.

- *The Heroine's Journey:* Immigrace is feminine. In several respects, the voice of the immigrant woman as a leader hasn't previously been clearly articulated. As immigration is celebrated, it is often done from a male perspective. Books such as *Immigrant, Inc.* highlight the stories of men who have boldly charted the course of freedom and who have, through their entrepreneurship, created bold American Dreams.

   As you read through the various stories in this book, you'll note that these women are on remarkable and beautiful journeys.

   Immigrace is not only about the journey to the United States (beyond the customs and migration borders, either by land, air, or sea), but also the journey each woman continues to embark upon as she moves through the oceans, peaks, valleys, highways, and byways of life in the United States. It's about living that genius, beyond the borders that life, systemic limitations or discrimination may place on us, as well as those we may unwittingly place on ourselves. The truth is, when we embrace our genius, there are no borders.

   You'll hear about each woman's journey from her unique, female perspective and how she's navigating life—the personal, professional, spiritual, and physical—and you'll hear how she brings forth the beautiful, bold, undeniable truth which she came to the United States and the world to express.

Each woman knows that her story is unique and unrepeatable. She takes full ownership of her entire journey—past, present, and future—who she is and where she is going.

- *Leadership:* Immigrace is a commitment to brilliance and excellence, to honing one's natural gifts, and to being a leader in the world. Mediocrity is not at all correlated with immigrace. In addition, immigrace is generous, humble, servant leadership.

- *Creativity:* Immigrace is putting things in the world that weren't previously there, or significantly improving things around us, and thereby putting a unique mark on families, industries, communities, and the world. Immigrace is life-giving and life-sustaining. A majority of the women profiled here are mothers, and hold dear their roles in bringing forth, nurturing, and sustaining new life.

- *Passionate:* Immigrace is embracing life with intense desire and enthusiasm and a sense of living it fully.

- *Beyond Brains:* Immigrace includes IQ, but expands beyond it to intuitive and emotional intelligence, with a knowledge of how to integrate the heart and the mind.

Immigrace permeates the entire book, and, as noted above, each chapter identifies the immigrace of each woman featured. We also explore creativity and innovation in more detail in part V. Here in part I, we meet three phenomenal women:

- Paola Prestini, artistic visionary, impresario, and trailblazer. Italy-born Paola is a successful music composer and producer in a male-dominated world. She shares what she learned from her mother's divorce shortly after the family's relocation to the United States. She also shares how a mentor radically redefined her professional path by teaching her the importance of being dedicated to her own art before helping those around her.

- Hsing-ay Hsu, concert pianist, educator, and producer. Born in China to a family of musicians, Hsing-ay reflects on the family's journey to America in search of religious freedom, the negative effects of pressures on Asian women to excel, and how the immigrant experience taught her to have difficult conversations.

- Bisila Bokoko, international businesswoman, entrepreneur, global leadership expert, and philanthropist. Spanish-born Bisila is the founder and CEO of BBES, a New York–based business development agency that represents, promotes and markets brands internationally. She shares about being a cultural hybrid, overcoming personal and professional challenges, and being the key to unlocking global potential for people and brands.

1.
Create
Your World

PAOLA PRESTINI
Artistic Visionary, Impresario, Trailblazer

Composer Paola Prestini's music seeks to explode the boundaries between interdisciplinary forms, in conversation with art, science, and social justice. She has collaborated with poets, filmmakers, and scientists in large-scale multimedia works that chart her interest in extra-musical themes ranging from the cosmos to the environment.

Her compositions have been commissioned and performed at the Brooklyn Academy of Music, Barbican Centre, Cannes Film Festival, Carnegie Hall, Chicago Symphony Orchestra, Kennedy Center, Los Angeles Philharmonic, and Los Angeles Opera, among others. She created the largest communal virtual reality opera with *The Hubble Cantata*, was part of the New York Philharmonic's legendary Project 19 initiative, and has written and produced large-scale projects like the eco-documentary *The Colorado*, narrated by Mark Rylance (premiered and commissioned by the Metropolitan Museum of Art and Houston DACAMERA series) and the lauded opera theater work *Aging Magician* (premiered and commissioned by the Walker Art

Center and the Krannert Center, with performances at Arizona State University, the New Victory Theater, and San Diego Opera).

Prestini is known for her genre- and glass-ceiling-breaking roles, including being the first woman in the New Works Initiative with her grand opera *Edward Tulane* (Minnesota Opera), and bringing artificial intelligence and disability visibility and impact together in the chamber opera *Sensorium Ex* (Atlanta Opera and Beth Morrison Projects for the Prototype Festival). In December 2020, she released *Con Alma,* an album and immersive digital event in collaboration with Mexican singer-songwriter Magos Herrera and more than thirty musicians around the world.

In January 2021, she joined the Kennedy Center and the Apollo Theater to launch *Active Hope,* a podcast that explores the role of artistic intellect and national strategic leadership at a pivotal moment for the arts.

Her upcoming works include piano concertos for Awadagin Pratt and A Far Cry, and for Lara Downes with the Louisville Orchestra, Oregon Bach Festival, and Ravinia Festival. Prestini is the cofounder and artistic director of the Brooklyn-based arts institution and incubator National Sawdust.

As part of her commitment to equity and mentoring the next generation of artists, she started the Hildegard Competition for emerging female, trans, and nonbinary composers and the Blueprint Fellowship for emerging composers with the Juilliard School. She was a Paul & Daisy Soros fellow and a Sundance fellow, has been in residence at the Park Avenue Armory and MASS MoCA, and is a graduate of the Juilliard School.

PAOLA AND I met for coffee in midtown NYC in 2013. I instantly loved her beautiful energy and warmth, as she took me on her exquisite journey of making music, creating magic, and illuminating new trails for herself and others. We have subsequently updated this chapter to reflect her current thoughts, eight years later.

Shattered Utopia

"It is the worst performance I've seen in my life."

With those ten words, Paola's idol, Philip Glass, had shattered her utopia. Glass is a world-renowned composer and pianist, who is widely recognized as one of the most influential composers of the twentieth century. Paola had observed his career for years and was thrilled when he agreed to attend her performance.

Paola had started her company as a nonprofit in her early twenties. She ran a collective of artists and was solely responsible for creating the infrastructure of the group. She and her consortium had worked hard on the performance, and Paola was convinced that performing for Glass was their big break. She was even more convinced of this when, after the show, Glass invited her to lunch. She went home thinking, *This is it! We made it!*

She nurtured a romantic view that running a collective was the way to go. Glass helped her see that the utopia she'd set up worked beautifully in principle, but much less so in reality: "You are carting around a troupe of people and not giving time to form yourself first," he said. He went on to tell her that until she dedicated herself to her art, she wouldn't be able to give fully to her artists or her community. And more importantly, she would not find her inner balance as a composer.

This feedback led to Paola's decision to take a year off to reflect on her business strategy. During her time out, she decided to reorganize her business. It's important to note that Glass did not become her mentor and that Paola did not adopt his specific business strategy. She went on to form her own works in VisionIntoArt, seminal works for which she is known, like *Oceanic Verses*, starring the muse, vocalist, and powerhouse Helga Davis, and *Aging Magician*, a work that premiered at the New Victory Theater on Broadway. However, she still commissions other artists. And years later, she started the Brooklyn-based incubator of music and ideas National Sawdust. What she took out of that conversation was that if she didn't take care of and nurture herself and her art, she couldn't holistically take care of others. It was the best and hardest lesson.

Paola turned her company into a production company and let go of the idea of a collective. In having her production company as her creative locus and epicenter, she was able to create a large part of her identity as composer and producer. This then grounded her when she went on to form an even larger venture, daresay a movement, in National Sawdust. With the benefit of several years behind her, Paola was grateful to Glass for this advice because it was a turning point for her, and for her understanding of what it takes to run a successful business.

Reeds of Transition and Separation

Paola migrated to the United States with her parents when she was two years old. The family moved to Nogales, Arizona, close to the Mexican border, because her dad made musical instruments and reeds. The cane for the reeds, the specific kind of cane Paola's father used, is predominantly found in southern France and northern Mexico. The Prestinis' decision to migrate to the United States was primarily a business decision, combined with the possibility of a new life, new opportunities, and new frontiers. Paola's mom was thrilled to be a new American and thrilled at all of the possibilities. She was filled with a sense of purpose and a sense that she had to do something with this opportunity.

The thrill was short-lived because soon after the relocation to the United States, her parents got divorced. Paola watched her mom struggle to raise her as a single parent. Her mom now carried two heavy dumbbells—the weights of being in a new country and of being newly single. These drove Paola's mom to offer Paola the best of everything—the best possible care, education, and upbringing. From her earliest years, Paola loved music and knew she wanted to be involved in music. Her mom did everything in her power to make that possible.

Sustainable Art

Paola left home at age sixteen to study music and hasn't looked back. She was committed to being a composer, but was also conscious of her place in the larger musical ecology. Paola is a recipient of the Paul & Daisy Soros Fellowship for New Americans. This was an important boost for Paola because she was surrounded by people who talked about sustainable business practices, people who, like Paola, were socially conscious. This was Paola's first clue that she was onto something important.

During her year as a Soros fellow, Paola was inspired to start her nonprofit. Her goal was to commission other artists, in order to create a positive context for having a career as a composer. She wanted sustainability in her career but also wanted to be able to sustain others and promote healthy business practices in the arts.

Most people give back at the end, or as they approach the end, of their careers. Paola didn't wait. In her twenties, she was already thinking about giving back, interdisciplinary practice, and what it means to be twenty-first-century artist. For Paola, being a twenty-first-century artist involves more than talent. It includes being an entrepreneur, an activist, and an educator. All those roles have taken her on a most interesting route as a musician and have formed and helped her grow her as an artist. She has taught music around the world—in NYC public schools, through El Sistema in Venezuela, in Mexico with Carnegie Hall, and through various residencies in Southern Italy.

An entrepreneur at heart, Paola loves the freedom of having her own company and promoting her own work and the work of other artists she admires. She is not constrained to do things in a particular way—flexibility and evolution are key. One of the challenges, of course, is that economically, you have to imagine and define your own world. Interdisciplinary work excites her. She is currently working with conservationists and is able to engage in deep, complex conversations that are illuminated by the arts. Paola views the arts as a tool to bring forward the truth about life, humanity, and what the world is and can be.

Paola now collaborates with the New York Philharmonic, the Los Angeles Philharmonic, the Brooklyn Academy of Music (BAM), and a number of world-renowned music houses. Paola has come a long way since the days when, along with her collective of artists, she began in a church basement on Seventy-First Street in New York. She credits failure and evolution and that early discussion with Glass in large part for challenging her entire paradigm early in her career.

A Trailblazer

There's a certain struggle in charting your own course. Paola is a trailblazing female in a field that is dominated, particularly at the most senior levels, by white males. In a 2014 article titled "Her Music: Today's Emerging Female Composer," WQXR cited the low numbers of female composers. According to Q2 Music, in the United States, women hold only 15 percent of composition faculty positions; women constitute under 15 percent of living composers whose works are featured on recent orchestral seasons and new-music series; in the history of prestigious composition prizes, women have received only 9 percent; and over half of the elite schools have no women on the composition faculty.[1] A 2019 article titled "Lenny Bernstein and Women Composers: The Bachtrack Classical Music Statistics for 2018" cited that the number of women composers whose works are featured in contemporary orchestral works increased to a staggering 16 percent.[2] Recall that the Q2 Music stated that this number was 15 percent in 2014. It only increased by a statistically insignificant 1 percent in four years.

Paola notes that the reasons for these low numbers are complex. There are conscious and unconscious biases at play in institutions. In addition, women are not encouraged to go into this kind of work. Women may not mentor other women. Paola sees a connection between creativity, innovation, and mentoring: "There is so little pie, and people often think about how to divide that pie instead of making more pie. We need to make more pie" (in the words of one of her mentors, Paul Soros). "We need to make more magic. And then we need to be trailblazers and mentor other women."

Create Your World

While growing up as an immigrant and through her work, Paola has been exposed to many different cultures and languages, and she values the importance of connecting cultures. Her mother worked all day and spoke Italian to her at night. Her nanny spoke Spanish to her. The nanny was supporting five children of her own.

Paola's mom owned and ran a children's store, and Paola learned from her mother that if you don't invest in your own company, no one else will. She watched as her mother saved up by working multiple jobs and then reinvested in her company. Today, Paola still believes in and practices the discipline of investing in yourself and your business.

Witnessing her mother's and her nanny's sacrifices taught her about motherhood. They also taught her about shaping the world around her. Paola's work is a manifestation of the world she wants to live in. When she commissions or considers programs, Paola asks, does this slice of life represent the life I want to live? Is it multiracial, is it multicultural, are there women? You have to create the world you want to live in.

Paola's Definition of Success

As Paola achieves certain standards of success in the industry, her own definition of success evolves. First, success requires being driven. This presupposes that one is driven by something—a mission, a passion, a calling, or a cause. Her definition of success is knowing who you are and fulfilling the goals you've set for yourself, while respecting yourself, your body, and your family. Often, when people are driven by causes and strong principles, it is challenging to find balance in the midst of the pursuit of excellence. This is especially true for women who are tasked with fulfilling their full potential as mothers, leaders, and entrepreneurs. Continually reevaluate your goals to make sure you are achieving balance while still striving.

PAOLA'S IMMIGRACE

- Artistic visionary
- Impresario
- Trailblazer

PAOLA'S IMMIGEMS

◇ *Don't follow in anyone's footsteps.* You can be guided and influenced by others' ideas, but you must be true to yourself and follow your own dreams. Paola recommends finding role models to emulate, but not seeking to be someone else. We must be clued into what our influences are, emotionally and intellectually, but the only recipe that works is that which you create for yourself.

Consider this: if you're walking on a beach, it is nearly impossible to follow someone else's footsteps exactly. This is a metaphor for our lives. You are a specific combination of past, present, and dream. The only way to fulfill your highest potential is to take the risks associated with those dreams.

◇ *Listen more to the noes.* When someone says no to Paola or tells her something is not possible, she hears that she has to find a way to make it a yes. She listens more to the noes than to the yeses. The noes become fascinating paths into new ways of thinking. Noes lead to moments of self-reflection, reevaluation, charting new paths, and ultimately growth.

◇ *Keep doors open.* Success can be overwhelming. As some gain success and become busier, they inadvertently or otherwise become less accessible. We all have a responsibility to help others. Make the time to help others. You never know what will illuminate a new path. Constantly reevaluate your time commitments, and weed things out. The moment you become inaccessible, you will lose touch with the things that got you there in the first place.

2.
Creativity and Wholeness

| **HSING-AY HSU**
Concert Pianist, Educator, and Producer

"Beijing-born, American-trained pianist Hsing-ay Hsu, with extraordinary prowess, breathes life into the music."
—*FANFARE MAGAZINE*

Since her stage debut at age four, Steinway Artist Hsing-ay Hsu (pronounced "Sing-I Shoo") has been performing at such venues as Carnegie Hall, the Kennedy Center, and Alice Tully Hall at Lincoln Center; in Europe and Asia; and at festivals including the International Keyboard Odyssiad & Festival and the Gulangyu International Piano Art Festival in China. Passionate about processing life through the human experience of music, Hsing-ay uses her rich experiences as a performer, studio owner, producer, consultant, clinician, and artist-teacher to help others make connections between analysis, emotions, and breath (mind/body/heart). She is especially interested in fostering multidisciplinary appreciation and teaching communications skills for musicians.

Hsing-ay's thoughtful musical interpretations have won her international recognition, including the William Petschek Debut

Award at Juilliard (highest honor given to a pianist), William Kapell International Competition, Ima Hogg National First Prize, Paul & Daisy Soros Fellowship, Gilmore Young Artist Award, and the US Presidential Scholar of the Arts Award from President Clinton. Her chamber music activities have included concerts from the intimate Bargemusic in New York to the Hong Kong Cultural Centre. An advocate of new music, she has recorded solo works of Ezra Laderman and premiered works by Ned Rorem. A versatile concerto soloist performing Bach to Barber, she is described by the *Washington Post* as full of "power, authority, and self-assurance." Concerto collaborations include the Houston Symphony Orchestra as first-prize winner of the Ima Hogg National Competition, Baltimore Symphony Orchestra, Colorado Symphony, Pacific Symphony (California), Colorado Springs Philharmonic, Florida West Coast Symphony, Fort Collins Symphony, New Jersey Symphony Orchestra, Waterbury Symphony Orchestra (Connecticut), China National Symphony Orchestra, Shanghai Symphony Orchestra, Shenzhen Symphony Orchestra, and Xiamen Philharmonic Orchestra.

Television and radio feature broadcasts include Garrison Keillor's *A Prairie Home Companion, Live from Tanglewood* (for more than ten thousand live audience members and a broadcast audience of 3.9 million), NPR's *Performance Today* with Martin Goldsmith, TCI Cablevision's Grand Piano Recital (California), WQXR's *Young Artists Showcase*, Colorado Public Radio's *Colorado Spotlight*, China Central National TV, Hong Kong Phoenix TV, and Danish National Radio. She has recorded CDs and DVDs for Pacific Records, Albany Records, and Nutmeg Press.

Hsing-ay is a multifaceted cultural collaborator and producer. During the COVID-19 pandemic, she began to release weekly offerings of interviews, performances, and musical concepts on her YouTube channel, *Hsing-ay Hsu*, and through her e-newsletter, "Hsing-ay's Notes." Previously the artistic director for Pendulum New Music at the University of Colorado Boulder for fourteen seasons, she brought in international artists to the region from Finland,

Mexico, and the UK, and she hosted master classes by celebrities including Kronos and Béla Fleck. She also copresented festivals of George Crumb and John Cage, created site-specific community outreach programming, and coached close to five hundred student composition premieres.

As owner of the Nutmeg Studio, Hsing-ay creates a retreat for creative lifelong learners like herself through lessons, coaching, workshops, and interactive listening webinars. She teaches master classes at such venues as Conservatoire Ravel in Paris and Xiamen University, and she adjudicates for national and international competitions. A beloved teacher, many of her students have won numerous solo and concerto prizes by gaining confidence through improving their daily practice. Besides chairing the Colorado State Music Teachers Association College Forum, she served on the national editorial board of *American Music Teacher* magazine. She has also taught as visiting piano faculty for several universities and organizations, including the University of Colorado Boulder and Friends of Chamber Music Denver, has lectured at conferences including the MTNA National Conference, and recently joined the faculty of the global online music studio Aeyons. Her Conscious Listening monthly seminars and dynamic Four-Step Method bring classical music to a wider audience through festivals, performances in private homes, music societies, and concert series talks. She also teaches every summer at the Rocky Ridge Adult Piano Seminars, the International Keyboard Odyssiad & Festival in Colorado, and Chautauqua's Special Studies in upstate New York.

Born in Beijing to a musical family, Hsing-ay trained with her uncle Fei-Ping Hsu, at the Juilliard School, and at Yale University, Aspen Music Festival and School, Ravinia's Steans Music Institute, the Aldeburgh Festival in the UK, and Tanglewood Music Center. Hsing-ay is married to composer Daniel Kellogg, who is the new president of Young Concert Artists, Inc., and they have one daughter. She is based in New York City. Besides music, she loves to travel with her family and take dance classes.

Hsing-ay shares blogs, newsletters, and videos at hsingayhsu. com. She releases YouTube videos on her channel, *Hsing-ay Hsu*.

HSING-AY AND I connected by email, and she enthusiastically agreed to speak about her immigrant journey. Although we spoke by phone, we instantly formed a bond, and her passion for creating beauty in the world through music was undeniable.

Daughter of Renewal

Hsing-ay was born shortly after Chinese Communist revolutionary and founder of the People's Republic of China, Mao Zedong, died. There had been hope that Mao's leadership would bring about long-desired stability in China, but the reverse was the case. Mao's ten-year Cultural Revolution was intended to wipe out old culture and all Western arts, to prolong the revolutionary spirit, and secure his personal power. Ten years of national trauma ensued, when anything cultural or intellectual was considered a threat to political powers, and was therefore suppressed. Education and creativity were strictly supervised and limited to propaganda purposes only.

Hsing-ay's grandfather was a pastor, and throughout his life in Communist China, he had been persecuted for his faith. Hsing-ay's parents, Fei-hsing Hsu and Jin-ay Liu, were well-respected musicians in the nation's capital. Fei-hsing was handpicked to play the concert for the US president's visit and for other national projects like creating the Yellow River Piano Concerto with a six-person committee. After Mao's death and the reopening of relationships with the West, Fei-hsing received one of a few US visas based on extraordinary talent. The United States held the promise of religious and individual freedoms and renewed hope for personal growth. The family was excited at the prospect of self-determination and the opportunity to create fuller identities for themselves, rather than having every aspect of their lives assigned to them, although it came at a time when artistic life in China was just starting to blossom again.

Hsing-ay's father decided to take the risk of moving, even though it meant giving up his successful professional career, and he relocated to New York, where his brother Fei-Ping Hsu was a star student at Juilliard. Two and a half years later, Hsing-ay and her mom eventually obtained visas and joined him in December 1984, selling all their possessions to pay for one-way plane tickets. Hsing-ay arrived in the United States, unconsciously carrying a "burden of hope" on her shoulders that had been accumulating for three years. Much of the family's future would be about creating opportunities for her. Even at such a young age, she felt that giving her best at all times was not only expected, but was also necessary to justify the family upheaval. While rising to immense challenges, inwardly she felt a lack of spiritual faith, financial resources, and the time required to fulfill all her ambitions. Acutely aware of her duty and family honor, and also of her strong intuition on all things musical, she was challenged to define what success actually meant in this new world.

That Elusive Dream

Soon after their arrival at New York's John F. Kennedy Airport, Hsing-ay and her parents began to suspect that the American Dream was more difficult to realize than they had imagined while they were in China. There was much uncertainty around their legal status, which meant her parents couldn't work for a period, and the family hit rock bottom financially. It was difficult to obtain solid advice on how to stay in the country legally. Hsing-ay's father found an "honorary position" as a staff pianist at a Bible college, where he performed to raise funds for the college in exchange for the administration's help to obtain a green card, which would allow him to start an application for citizenship. However, after years without progress, he began to wonder whether the college was actually processing any paperwork at all. Hsing-ay's parents had given up secure jobs as China's A-list artists at the best venues, had sold everything they owned, and had to depend on the help of many friends to make the arduous transition; now, returning to China after so much sacrifice loomed as a daunting and genuine possibility.

Those years of struggle strengthened Hsing-ay's nuclear family. They leaned on one another for emotional support. Without a network of concert presenters, they created an unusual patchwork life. The road trips for church concerts made for fine bonding time over long drives, as did rehearsing together. Hsing-ay learned how to take big risks from her dad, and she learned from her mom how to be resourceful and to always ask lots of questions, two skills that have been vital for her music career.

Little Outsider

"They own different sweaters for every day of the week!"

This sudden realization ran a rather sizeable highlighter across the differences between Hsing-ay and the other kids at school. Other kids at her American elementary school changed outfits each day, while she wore the same sweater all winter!

Although Hsing-ay counts having access to such excellent education as a blessing, she didn't fit in with the other children. She was a Chinese immigrant in the midst of Caucasian children. In China, her family had been considered well-off, and a single sweater was a wonderful possession. But in this little wealthy town in New Jersey, they were suddenly considered poor, not having the same financial resources as their neighbors.

All the other kids obsessed over sports, but Hsing-ay didn't even know what the rules were. Her parents had been two of China's top classical musicians, and Hsing-ay was considering a career in their footsteps. None of her classmates had the foggiest idea what classical music was, nor did they care. While the social aspect of school was awkward, there were at least class-wide birthday parties to attend. Other than stressing about how to afford buying so many presents, she was always excited to attend these eye-opening cultural highlights and got a taste for event planning, which planted a seed for an interest in producing concerts later on.

Being an outsider did not prevent her from making an impact or discovering what she could contribute. Two highlights from her school days were the day her struggling classmate passed his biology dissection orals because of her tutoring, and the day her high school student government presented her with The Spirit Award for making the community a better place. There were also several hidden benefits of accepting that she did not socially belong at an early age. She loved her solitude, had time to daydream for hours, and developed an immunity to peer pressure. She also treasured her freedom to choose her values from among two diverse cultures and her ability to understand both cultures' perspectives on the same issues.

Patterns of Discrimination

Hsing-ay's encounters with discrimination in the United States were initially confounding to her. For a young Communist girl, who was raised on the firm belief that the authority acted for the good of the people, she had a hard time understanding the strange behaviors of authority figures in the United States. One such example was when her history teacher, also a minority, gave her a lower grade than her female Caucasian classmate. Hsing-ay had responded correctly to the question that was presented. In comparing her response to that of her classmate, there was no objective reason for Hsing-ay to receive a lower grade. Hsing-ay reached out to her teacher to better understand this disconnect. He simply stated, "I expected more from you."

Similar moments have occurred during the course of Hsing-ay's life in the United States, but she didn't realize that the double standard of "judging Asians more harshly" could be part of a broader pattern of discrimination until the Harvard University admissions lawsuit made headlines. Students for Fair Admissions, representing a group of Asian American students rejected by Harvard University, sued Harvard for assigning lower personality points to Asians, as a way to reduce the number of Asians being admitted. Although the plaintiffs lost the initial lawsuit and appeal, the decisions acknowledged the existence of the practice. The case is expected to go to the United States Supreme Court.[1]

Another example of strange behavior exhibited by an authority figure at school was when Hsing-ay signed up to run for student council president. She wanted to make a difference in the student community. The other candidate was a popular jock who didn't care much about policies. The election supervisor was an athletics coach and, firmly assuming an introverted minority girl's inevitable loss to a popular, great-looking guy, called the debate off entirely and invited Hsing-ay to do something symbolic, such as taking on the role of secretary instead. These experiences are not uncommon among immigrants, who leave certain barriers, such as religious persecution, in their home countries but experience barriers of a different kind in the United States, such as racial and other forms of discrimination.

Musical Companion

Hsing-ay was an only child, but music was her ever-present sibling and friend. Her family played church music all across the United States, spending days in the homes of generous Christian families. They got to meet numerous American families. Music brought Hsing-ay's family so much joy, and expressing that joy without censorship was heartening.

Since both Hsing-ay's parents were pianists, she always had access to a piano. Her father had performed as part of the Central Philharmonic, the national symphony in Beijing, so there was an upright piano in the family's apartment. Her mom was both a pianist and the harpist at the Central (Western) Opera. Hsing-ay was never forced to play, but being surrounded by instruments and watching her parents play led to her exploration and love of piano. Music was her way of processing life.

The Myth of Perfection

In the world of music, concert pianists are especially prone to expectations of perfection.

"Love over perfection" is Hsing-ay's heartfelt advice to Chinese and other immigrant women and musicians who struggle with the myth of perfection. "We must learn to put our self-worth on love, loving others, and being loved, and not on being perfect," she says.

The standard of perfection goes something like this: you are expected to do your best at everything, and your best is supposed to be perfect, worthy only of praise, and beyond reproach or criticism.

As immigrant women strive for excellence in the United States, navigating expectations of perfection is a prominent challenge. Hsing-ay notes that in many Asian cultures, everyone is expected to conform to the rules and measure up to a social standard. These days, the Chinese government is imposing a social score based on citizens' behavioral conformity.

There are positives and negatives to this cultural perspective. One positive is being part of a strong community and having the community's support. Another positive is the desire for self-improvement. Hsing-ay's name means "always growing." This is a very typical Chinese concept—the never-ending quest to improve and get to the next level.

But there is also a culture of shame. What others in the community think about you is important, so one's sense of self and identity are intertwined with that of the community and what the community thinks. Brené Brown describes perfectionism as "the belief that if we live perfect, look perfect, and act perfect, we can minimize or avoid the pain of blame, shame, or judgment. It is a shield."[2]

These expectations of perfection are unrealistic, and the quest to please others is fatiguing and becomes a stumbling block. Many women experience lower self-esteem when faced with the reality of imperfection.

Another obstacle is misaligned values. For instance, the world of pianists, like many other fields, favors "dominating values" such as stamina, quantity, volume, strength, oversized halls, and confident and assertive personas. Hsing-ay, like other sensitive artists, is an intuitive and gentle soul who has worked hard to convince the masculine-values-dominated juries, faculties, and managers that she is as tough and aggressive as any male competitor.

Yet immigrant women in the United States must remember that we all have the opportunity to define success for ourselves and place less value on others' negative judgment of us. Conversely, we can put less value on accolades, understanding that our inherent value doesn't rest in them. As we immigrant women explore our unique gifts, talents, and how we choose to serve, in loving ourselves and loving others as Hsing-ay recommends, we can continue to authentically express our true values in this beautiful, imperfect world.

Immeasurable Gifts

Part of the beauty Hsing-ay sees in the world is in exploring her mind through music, and she never tires of it. As she evolves as a musical artist, she's come to love the clarity of music. Creativity forces you to think about your work, and there is excitement in being intentional about the very act of thinking.

Hsing-ay is passionate about how creative work affects thinkers in any field. The obsession with measuring what we produce is inapt as it relates to music because much of the beauty of music is in emotional discovery. The measuring is also counterproductive, as it can limit our ability to step back, innovate, and create.

Central to our creativity is the importance of protecting the very space where ideas can flourish. Hsing-ay notes that: "Each of us, regardless of who we are or what we do, must understand the importance of making and allowing time for creativity. We need to set aside time to think, reflect, listen, and allow our creativity to unfold."

Through music, we can connect with a composer of a different time and language. Hsing-ay is a translator of sorts, translating the emotions and messages of composers from years and times past to audiences today.

The world of classical and concert music is also being threatened by other forms of leisure and entertainment. Performers need to invest in outreach and education to protect this form of artistic expression. Over the years, Hsing-ay has incorporated teaching and outreach into her work. She focuses on adults who share her passion for lifelong learning. She has also created Conscious Listening workshops, which tap into the emotions and multiple perspectives. She has led outreach classes accompanied by concerts, which include teaching the class how to listen and attend concerts together. At the University of Colorado Boulder, where she was the artistic director of Pendulum New Music, she taught the composers and performers how to listen to each other's intentions and needs, and she brought in international and national artists to inspire the community.

She's also homeschooled her daughter, whose instruction incorporated many creative extracurricular activities, and doing so allowed her to protect her daughter's creative time. During the pandemic, she started producing weekly broadcasts, titled "Processing Life through Music," on her YouTube channel, *Hsing-ay Hsu*, with a variety of content, from performance with commentary to musical breathwork. She is launching online courses and creating new collaborations.

Hsing-ay has redefined her career over the years, from just playing to incorporating teaching and producing and now innovating new ways to promote the importance of creativity. Her quest is to offer music as a space for awareness, making connections, and finding wholeness, and she joins the movement of creating a gentler and more creative world.

Hsing-ay's Definition of Success

Success is "the process of identifying potential in people and things, having a vision of how to develop that potential, and carrying it forward over a long-term commitment. Ruth Bader Ginsburg believed that lasting change happens in incremental steps. There is so much expectation and anger ripe for instant revolution these days, but I hope we can find the patience to be part of committed movements that will live past us."

HSING-AY'S IMMIGRACE

- Inspirational performer and life commentator: making deep connections
- Compassionate educator: making space for multiple perspectives and finding an abundance of paths forward

HSING-AY'S IMMIGEMS

◇ *Listen for emotions.* Create meaningful bonds that enable us to move things forward. Hsing-ay is curious about why people feel the way they do. She seeks out clues and doesn't allow assumptions to color her lenses. Listening is a skill, and we must be attentive to when people don't feel safe, when something is triggering to them, or when they don't feel heard. Sometimes listening to all the different voices within ourselves can be the most challenging. Differentiating between voices that haunt us from our past and voices that speak truth in the present moment is also crucial to our understanding of the world.

◇ *Have the difficult conversations, no matter how uncomfortable they are.* Growing up as an immigrant, Hsing-ay often saw people seek to take advantage of her parents and their lack of social resources, which led to many uncomfortable conversations about how to balance seeking justice versus seeking safety. These situations taught her to stand up and speak up for herself and to address the uncomfortable subjects that many would much rather avoid.

◇ *Let go of the who gets the credit.* As a woman and minority, Hsing-ay sometimes felt invisible or passed over and had feared not being fairly recognized or compensated for her work and time. In order for leadership to work, you can't be caught up in questions of who gets the credit. In her experience, moving the program or project forward needs to be the first priority, and getting credit is not a worthwhile distraction. "This takes a lot of trust that my work will speak for itself to the people that really matter. Navigating this includes being at ease about secondary issues. After developing a good track record of success, the credit will either catch up, or there will emerge a pattern of being continually taken for granted by leadership. The bigger the organization, the more distant we may feel to the organization's priorities. Finding the right questions to ask and constantly re-confirming our reading of the context is so crucial. If credit is not given, it is a helpful indicator that we need to dig deeper to find the disconnect and plan our next moves!" She is grateful to her teachers and mentors for their guidance, as well as the generations of men and women whose work have made her own life in music possible.

3.
The Dream Factory

| **BISILA BOKOKO**
| International Businesswoman, Entrepreneur,
| Global Leadership Expert, and Philanthropist

Considered one of the ten most influential Spanish women in American business, and declared "an international change agent" by *Black Enterprise*, Bisila Bokoko is an acclaimed businesswoman, entrepreneur, and philanthropist.

Based in New York City, Bisila is a United Nations–award-winning entrepreneur and global leadership speaker and expert. She hails from Spain, with roots in Equatorial Guinea. She is the founder and CEO of Bisila Bokoko Embassy Services (BBES), a consultancy firm, as well as Bisila Wines & Cavas. Since 2009, her nonprofit organization, the Bisila Bokoko African Literacy Project (BBALP), has opened libraries in Ghana, Zimbabwe, Kenya, and Uganda.

As the executive director of the Spain-US Chamber of Commerce for seven years, she worked closely with leading Spanish brands, including Agatha Ruiz de la Prada, Zara, Mango, and Desigual, to facilitate their US market entry.

Bisila's efforts have won her widespread global recognition and numerous prestigious awards, and they also led to her involvement with Empretec, a United Nations Conference on Trade and Development program that supports up-and-coming entrepreneurs. She has held the esteemed positions of chair of the executive board and annual host of their Women in Business Awards since 2010.

From hosting at the World Investment Forum in Switzerland to delivering powerful keynotes in the Dominican Republic and radio hosting in South Africa, Bisila has shared her holistic business expertise and impacted individuals and organizations the world over. "BB" is notorious for taking companies from local to global and advising world leaders.

With her international business expertise and impeccable style, Bisila has graced the covers of fashion magazines such as *Vogue España*. She has also been featured in *Forbes Africa, Forbes Woman, Vanity Fair, Entrepreneur, Glamour, Harper's Bazaar,* and *Black Enterprise* and on Bloomberg TV. She has written and shared leadership insights for the Huffington Post and Thrive Global.

Throughout her twenty-year career, Bisila has developed and cultivated relationships with international business leaders and heads of state such as Queen Sofía of Spain.

Bisila earned an MBA in business administration and economics in Madrid from San Pablo University and holds an MA in international relations from the City College of New York. She also obtained a certificate of British law at the University of Manchester.

BISILA IS A powerhouse global businesswoman and leader who I'm proud to call a beloved sister and friend. She is deeply passionate about making a magnificent impact on our world. Embracing and leveraging her bicontinental origins (Africa and Europe), and from her home in the heart of New York City, she helps governments, businesses, and leaders—particularly women leaders—to tap into their fullest potential by sharing incisive business strategies, as well as the rarest of wisdom and profound life lessons.

A Blended Cocktail

Where are you from? This rather simple question is sometimes a complicated one for immigrants to answer. *Do you mean where I was born, or where I live?* In Bisila's case, it seems particularly tricky because when she tells people she is from Spain, considering that she was born in Valencia, they often don't believe her and request further clarification. Was she was adopted, or was she a refugee to Spain? Are there even Black people in Spain? She offers clarification, such as the fact that her parents are from Equatorial Guinea in Africa. At other times, people assume she is African American, until they hear her distinct Spanish accent. They then assert that she sounds like she is from Brazil, Costa Rica, or the Caribbean. Part of the challenge is that people want her to choose one of these identities or locations—a single identity is required in order to fit the mold and their perception of her. But Bisila rejects and defies being placed in a single, limited, and narrowly defined box.

Bisila believes that cultural identity is an integral part of who we are, our human development, and how we engage with others. For her, it is essential to get this right, both for herself and for others. In the end, she feels most "at home" with herself when she puts all these cultures together and creates a happy cocktail, as she calls it. She celebrates her rich background by describing herself as a cultural hybrid, that is, one who's internalized two or more different belief systems and feels comfortable in all of them. Cultural hybrids also have the ability to switch between common behaviors in those distinct cultures. This framing as a cultural hybrid also instantly signals to people that Bisila has a more intricate identity. It isn't a simple view; it's expansive, global, and expresses the infinite potential of humanity.

Bisila also views her varied cultural background as a strength and as a key to opening doors of understanding and unlocking massive value creation. Her Spanish birth and upbringing opens doors, not only in Spain but in Europe as a whole. Her native Spanish-speaking skills also open doors in Latin America. Being a daughter of Africa opens doors on the African continent and in the diaspora. As a New Yorker for decades, she is American. Once she embraced those three continents, she understood herself to be a global citizen, and a love for Asian and Eastern cultures naturally developed. This understanding has also led to a deep sense of self-acceptance.

A Dream Fulfilled

Bisila visited the United States for vacation in 1999, and she fell in love with New York City. She decided it was where she wanted to live. While she had nurtured a dream to live in the United States since her earlier years, as young as four or five years old, visiting New York crystallized it. Bisila is one of the most determined people I know, so what followed after this was not at all surprising. She found out that her company also had an office in New York, and she obtained the opportunity for a transfer through an internship program. By 2000, she was living in NYC.

The initial transition was tough because she had come to the United States alone, and she soon became miserable. NYC was a fast-paced, aggressive, and dirty place. She'd left friends and family at home in Spain and only had coworkers as companions. She called her three brothers constantly. She was in her twenties and didn't feel prepared for the separation and isolation that led to moments of despair.

There were also some genuine financial challenges. There were real estate brokers who took advantage of her ignorance as a new immigrant and took large sums of money as upfront payments for apartments. The apartments in question were mice-ridden and nowhere close to the quality she'd grown accustomed to back home in Spain.

There were days when she seriously considered returning permanently to Spain. But she was driven by her determination to succeed in NYC and didn't want to be one who gave up on the American Dream and returned home.

Another significant challenge was adjusting her visa to permanent status. She'd come to the United States for an internship but had decided to remain in NYC. Unfortunately, there were a number of restrictions on her J-1 visa. She describes this chapter of her life as a nightmare, which included spending thousands of dollars on immigration attorneys. There was also an episode where she was detained in a room at John F. Kennedy Airport in New York, following one of her visits to Spain. The lengthy and aggressive questioning centered around why she kept coming in and out of the country so much. She was relieved when this chapter was finally behind her.

Entrepreneurship Chose Her

Some graduates jump right into professional ivory towers and set about climbing the ladder in their industry of choice. After Bisila completed her undergraduate studies in Spain, she initially felt lost and a sense of crisis, unsure of what she wanted to do with those degrees. She worked with her father, who was an attorney, but she decided it wasn't for her. She then worked as a legal assistant at Carbo & Martinez Law in Valencia. Realizing that the practice of the law was different from her initial impressions of it, she decided against pursuing a career in law.

When she began to learn more about international business, it ignited a spark within her—she loved the idea of helping people achieve their dreams. She wanted to be part of the entrepreneurial voyages and help people share their gifts with the world.

After her role at the law firm, Bisila worked for the Valencia Institute of Export (IVEX). It was through IVEX that she came to NYC as an intern. Following her decision to remain in NYC after her internship was over, she enrolled at the City College of New York in 2001, and obtained a master's degree in 2003.

IVEX subsequently promoted her to director, where she helped Spanish businesses across industries—ranging from food and lifestyle goods to beverages and spirits—to enter the US market. In 2005, the Spain-US Chamber of Commerce hired her, eventually promoting her to executive director.

Then came one of the greatest educational experiences of her life. One fateful day in 2012, she was called into an office and was fired. She had two young children, and she was going through a divorce. This was a most terrifying chapter in her life. She had lost the security of her paycheck, her employer's identity, her professional title, and her marriage—all in the same week.

She traveled to Spain to spend some time with her family and gain some perspective. Although she had been exposed to various entrepreneurs through her work at the Chamber of Commerce, she hadn't had the courage to jump into entrepreneurship with both feet. Getting fired shoved her into it. She decided to form her own company, BBES. And she was resolute. Seven days later, she had her first client.

Her various experiences working for companies taught her well, but she believes entrepreneurship is fate: "I am a rebel," she says. "If I go back to working for someone else, I may get fired again."

The Dream Factory

With her brother as her business partner, in 2010 she started her wine business, Bisila Wines & Cavas. Those early years with the wine company introduced her to entrepreneurship through some lessons in failure. The wine business lost $100,000 in three years, including all their initial investments and personal savings. The company subsequently found its stride and partnered with another winery, Ladrón de Lunas. Today, Bisila Wines makes red, white, and sparkling wines, with China as their largest consumer market, followed by Germany.

Being an entrepreneur has enabled Bisila to live her dreams, wearing multiple hats as a speaker, entrepreneur, leadership strategist, winemaker, and mentor. She is a bit of a gypsy as well. She travels the world and can work from anywhere. She may be in Geneva on one day and Cape Town on the next. During the coronavirus pandemic, she innovated by launching her YouTube channel, *BB Knows Best*, through which she shares leadership insights and conversations with business leaders and entrepreneurs in English and Spanish.

Being an entrepreneur has also enabled Bisila to be a voice and global ambassador. She holds a key and opens the doors to new markets. Through BBES, she helps take companies from local to global. She is a facilitator and ambassador for local Spanish companies in the fields of fashion, lifestyle, arts, and culture, helping them strengthen their brands for global impact. She has helped artists, singers, and other entrepreneurs from Spain to live their impossible dreams of bringing their talents and services to the United States, with performances at world-renowned arenas such as Madison Square Garden.

As an example, the Liceu Barcelona Opera House US Foundation appointed Bisila global ambassador. Simultaneously, Queen Sophía of Spain accepted the honorary presidency of the foundation's board of trustees. Bisila helped orchestrate a gala in New York City, which was attended by the queen and other members of the board of trustees, as well as potential patrons and other Spanish entrepreneurs based in New York City.

Her services have led to an extensive clientele from around the world, and thus Bisila has become a factory of dreams, helping others create, forge, and live their impossible dreams on global stages.

Bisila is a voracious reader, consuming multiple books every month. Books have therefore been the centerpiece of her philanthropic efforts through BBALP. The project fosters literacy in Africa by building well-equipped, modern, and sustainable and efficient libraries with the aim of sharing the gift of ideas and education in rural communities across Africa. The first library was built in Kokofu, Ghana, in 2010. BBALP currently has operations in Zimbabwe, Kenya, and Uganda.

Bisila's Definition of Success

Success is what makes you jump out of bed, even when you are not paid for it. It's not what you are doing, but who you are being. It is not what you do for applause or what people say about you. When you are able to define who you are, independent of the applause or others' opinions, then you are truly free and truly successful.

BISILA'S IMMIGRACE

- International businesswoman and entrepreneur
- Global leadership expert and speaker
- Philanthropist

BISILA'S IMMIGEMS

◇ *Remember that you are whoever you believe you are.* You are the decision maker. If you have confidence and a positive sense of yourself, your life will unfold according to that belief. If you believe the contrary, your life and results will also reflect this.

◇ *Escape the ego and be of service.* If you influence others in a positive way, you also benefit, but it is best when you come from the perspective of selfless service.

◇ *Take care of your heart-set, soul-set, and mindset.* There will be hardship along the way, but the only way to navigate through it is if your heart is in the right place, coming from a place of love; your soul is on fire through prayer, meditation, and spiritual fuel; and your mindset is optimal.

Immigrace Journal

Say Yes to Your Immigrace: *Discover Your Genius*

1. Who do I want to be in the world?

   _____

   _____

2. What dreams have been entrusted to me? What are some things I believe in my gut that I'm meant to do in this world? (It could be one thing, or it could be ten.)

   _____

   _____

3. What are three things I enjoyed doing as a child?

   _____

   _____

4. What are three activities that make me feel creative?

   _____

   _____

5. What activities do I get lost in? What can I do for hours without realizing the passage of time? These don't have to be careers or professional activities.

_____

_____

_____

6. If no one (including me) could talk me out of it, what three possible careers paths would I follow?

_____

_____

_____

7. In what areas of my life am I living my genius?

   a. Three activities that represent living my genius professionally:

   _____

   _____

   _____

   b. Three activities that represent living my genius personally:

   _____

   _____

   _____

8. What new, higher expression of me is waiting to be brought to life?

_____

_____

_____

9. I commit to doing these three things to develop my genius over the next three months:

   _____

   _____

   _____

10. Who can support me in nurturing my genius? (Think mentor, coach, or teacher.)

    _____

    _____

    _____

11. My purpose in this world is:

    _____

    _____

    _____

12. The grandest vision of my life includes:

    _____

    _____

    _____

PART II
Inner Self-Mastery
Find Joy

Immigrants often excel at looking great on paper. Consider the following educational statistics: according to a January 2018 study by the New American Economy, Sub-Saharan African immigrants were significantly more likely to hold graduate degrees, with 16 percent having a master's degree, medical degree, law degree, or doctorate, compared with 11 percent of the US-born population.[1]

According to a 2017 US Census Bureau study of select immigrant populations from countries in Africa and the Caribbean, Nigerians had the highest educational attainment at 61.4 percent, followed by Ethiopians (27 percent), Trinidadians and Tobagonians (25.7 percent), Jamaicans (24.8 percent), and Haitians (19.2 percent).[2]

I believe education is a powerful tool for personal development and transformation. I was born on a university campus and I come from a family of pioneering educators. My father was a professor, and my mother obtained her master's degree a few years after I was born. She also obtained her PhD much later in life, after all five of us (her children) had obtained graduate degrees.

We lived on three university campuses—the one where I was born; a second, when my father helped cofound a new university in eastern Nigeria; and a third when the same university relocated to a different town in eastern Nigeria.

My grandfather (my mother's father) was also a pioneering educator and renowned headmaster (principal). He founded schools across eastern Nigeria and valued education highly.

As the statistics suggest, Nigerians place a high premium on education. The Igbos, my ethnic group within Nigeria, are also often associated with high achievement, resilience, and enterprising spirits.

Although my siblings and I obtained undergraduate and graduate degrees at Harvard, Stanford, Oxford, and two from Yale, my parents never pushed us towards specific achievements. The intellectuals around us, including uncles, aunts, family friends, and others, set high standards. Through osmosis, excellence was understood, expected, and demanded.

While I believe such high achievement and resilience are commendable to some degree, I have often referred to it as part of the traditional immigrant success story—looking great on paper, but not necessarily being happy on the inside. I recognize it because I've lived it.

A number of years after law school, I was working late on the twenty-seventh floor of a tall building. It was probably about 8:30 at night, and I asked myself: *All of that was for this? Is this really all there is? The four hours of sleep almost every night while I worked part-time in college, the heavy law school textbooks, the frigid Cambridge, Massachusetts, winters, and the long hours of study at the Langdell law library at Harvard. All of that was for this?*

I was making what seemed like a lot of money, but I was in debt. I left the large law firm because working in-house was supposed to be less stressful for me as a working wife and mother, but I still experienced a high degree of stress. The problem wasn't the really long hours; the problem was that I didn't feel happy or fulfilled. I was living the lie of the traditional immigrant success story.

I wanted to be happy and fulfilled, and I wasn't either of those. An important turning point was reading John Maxwell's *The 21 Irrefutable Laws of Leadership*. I've described this as the beginning of my leadership and self-development journey. It wasn't so much a journey to discover something outside of myself as it was a journey to rediscover the joy I considered—and still consider—to be an integral part of who I am. I still believe joy is a super power and one of the greatest lies of adulthood is that stress is an integral part of being a grown-up. We must continually discover, rediscover, and defend our joy.

This self-awareness and self-development journey has now evolved into a commitment to be better on the inside than I look on paper or on the outside.

What's in a Name?

In a certain sense, I started in the middle because I shared the meaning of my middle name, but haven't shared the meaning of my first name. Chinwe means God's own.

My parents were certainly up to something when they chose this name. For context, Chinwe is one of the most common names in Igbo, my Nigerian language. Usually, however, it's Chinwendu (God owns life), Chinwenwa (God owns the child), Chinweaku (God owns wealth), etc. My parents took a bold stance and called me Chinwe period, with no qualifier, declaring that God owns me. This is a truth that has proven itself over and over in my life and one that I hold very dear. Igbos have also maintained the concept of the "chi" as the personal spirit or the soul of a person, representing an inextricable link between the human the the divine.

The name is therefore relevant to the immigrace conversation for two reasons. First, depth of the meaning of this name is part of the reason I consistently disregarded the misguided advice to change my name to an English or more "Americanized" name. I strongly urge immigrant women not to discard this critical piece of their identity in a quest to fit into American society. Your uniqueness is an asset. As you will note from all the women featured here, none of them cited "changing their names" as immigems, nor have they credited it as a success strategy. Immigrant women leaders do not come into the United States—indeed, we do not come into this world—to blend in; we are here to shine.

Second, when I first embarked on this project, I didn't expect faith to be one of the prominent themes in the book. As it turns out, most of the women featured in this book believe in God. You'll note stories of Christians, Jews, and Muslims. You'll also note that Buddhists and various other forms of spirituality are represented here. One common theme is fleeing religious and other forms of oppression in other countries and coming to the United States in search of freedom. In addition, the spiritual aspect of our lives, varied though they may be, is a uniting theme and a key component of inner self-mastery and finding joy.

Joy as a Superpower

Joy and happiness are closely related. Joy is sometimes defined as: a state of happiness, felicity, or bliss; the emotion of great delight or happiness caused by something exceptionally good or satisfying; keen pleasure or elation. Happiness is often defined as a feeling of pleasure or contentment.

Happiness is primarily an emotional state. It is possible to have joy, and not feel the emotion of happiness. It is also possible to pursue inauthentic happiness—the emotion for its own sake, without regard for how such happiness impacts us (or those around us) in the long run.

Joy, as used throughout this book, is intended to describe, not only a joyful feeling, but something deeper, even spiritual, and includes not only desiring one's own good in the short and long run, but also the good of others.

Radical Ownership

In order to live fulfilled lives, we must take full ownership for every aspect of our journeys—past, present, and future. The concept of radical ownership is one of the most challenging ideas I know.

We tend to have clear ideas about what others could do differently. But the clouds and fog show up when it relates to what *we* can do differently. A perfect example for me was in the area of my relationship and being very clear about what my husband needed to do differently. It was only when I understood the idea of 100 percent ownership, not 50/50, that something truly shifted. One hundred percent ownership involves taking full responsibility for our lives and all our outcomes. The reason this is important is that once you can attribute blame to someone or something other than yourself, you are by definition stating that you are powerless to change your circumstances.

I first began to hone this skill when I worked with coaches who challenged me to see my own blind spots. I hated it. But today, I actively seek these blind spots out because I know understanding and addressing those blinds spots allows authentic growth to happen.

Ownership does not equal blame. The difference between ownership and guilt is that ownership empowers and guilt disempowers.

Radical ownership means that we own all of our experiences, especially the failures, mistakes, and points of pain. We have to be able to tell ourselves the truth.

Once we take ownership, first by cleaning up the crevices, then we can build whatever inner edifice we want—we can create a castle, a mansion, a cottage, or cabin. Then we must continually take care of our hearts, minds, and souls by doing the inner work and using various tools to support ourselves.

Healthy Resilience

I first heard of the concept of toxic strength from Dr. Claire J. Green-Forde, licensed clinical social worker, during a conversation on racism and mental health, following the tragic killing of George Floyd in 2020. It begins with the idea that people of certain backgrounds or ethnicities can endure an incredible number of difficulties. It's a belief that what doesn't kill you makes you stronger. It's being told, for example, that you are a strong Black woman, but the strength doesn't give you permission to be soft, needy, held, or comforted. It doesn't give you permission to be supported. It is the expectation that you can be knocked down over and over and over and not give yourself permission to stay down for a while, to mourn, to be scared, to be tender, to be vulnerable, to process, to be comforted. You're attributed a strength that doesn't allow for any of this. This is why it is toxic, or simply stated, unhealthy.

There's a powerful TEDx Talk by Tammie Denyse, titled "Toxic Strength," which is an excellent watch to learn more about this topic. She shares the story about how people expected her to be strong when her son was murdered in gun violence.

This concept of toxic strength is also applicable to immigrants. People often attribute strength and resilience to immigrants. Resilience is mental toughness, elasticity, and the ability to recover quickly from setbacks—being able to bounce back to normal or emerge stronger after a setback. It is the ability to keep going and thriving under all circumstances.

Resilience is an excellent leadership attribute. But it can have negative aspects. One negative aspect of resilience, is when it becomes a reason not to properly process tragic events or trauma in our lives. I'm no psychologist, but life experience has taught me that it is incredibly important that we process our emotions, and it's of utmost importance that we process the trauma. Mastering our emotions is key to living fulfilled and joyful lives. My favorite tool used to be avoidance: *If I ignore this long enough, it'll go away and it won't steal my joy*, I'd think. I've since replaced this with the practice of proactively addressing challenges. This is healthy resilience and the results are far better.

The problem with not addressing negative events, emotions, and experiences is that they often get worse, or those emotions are expressed in different or more problematic ways. Moment-to-moment acknowledgment of what we are feeling, and the overall management of our state, is critical to our emotional well-being and happiness.

Another negative application of resilience can be moving on too soon from challenges without pausing to learn the lessons. The Hogan Leadership Scales explore the potentially negative aspects of leadership. When faced with high-pressure situations, leaders' strengths can become success derailers. Leaders go over to the "dark side," so to speak. Drive becomes ruthless ambition, and attention to detail becomes micromanaging.

As it relates to resilience, some (myself included, as confirmed when I took the Hogan test) have an inclination to move on too quickly when there's a problem. Moving on too quickly is in contrast to ruminating or dwelling on and evaluating the worst-case scenario. The risk in moving on too quickly is that we could miss out on the juicy lessons those challenges present.

Regardless of where you are on the resilience scale and your overall tendencies, take the time to find those hidden lessons. Some lessons will become apparent over time, but thoughtfully considering the lessons when faced with the setback will help uncover nuggets while the facts are still fresh.

Set New Standards of Brilliance—At Home

Most of us immigrant women were raised in societies and cultures where there are certain defined roles and expectations of women, specifically in the household. These expectations of what being a wife and mother entails follow us to the United States. We want to hold strongly to our cultural heritage. We want to do our parents and ancestors proud. The problem is that we sometimes create expectations that are unrealistic and also lead to a high degree of stress and contribute to overwhelm and burnout.

They are unrealistic in part because a lot of these standards were set in different times and contexts. Our mothers and grandmothers lived in societies with strong extended families and support systems.

They didn't live the realities a lot of American wives and mothers do today. Some of us navigate back-to-back conference calls from 7:00 a.m. to 7:00 p.m., with very few breaks in-between. Others are single mothers raising boys in suburban communities. Today's virtual workplaces increasingly encroach on personal time. The pandemic has also made people more isolated than ever.

With the realities of our day, we must set new standards of brilliance—standards of brilliance that make sense and are attainable. Standards that support our mental health, our well-being, and our joy. This means we must start by telling ourselves the truth. We must have honest conversations with our spouses and family support systems about division of labor and how the household goals will be accomplished.

The challenge is perhaps even more dire for single mothers, who have to be thoughtful about responsibilities and what appropriate support could look like. For immigrant women, it's most important to let go of standards that were created in entirely different societies and contexts.

This section is about seeking joy in the midst of hardship, and in it, we will hear the stories of three women who have encountered great tragedy. They share what they've learned and are learning from those experiences and how they continue to find joy. They speak about grief, tragedy, war, refugee camps, death, and how we can move through such experiences with grace. They talk about faith, and how that journey may include rough spots, as we encounter life's challenges and tragedies.

This section includes the stories of:

- Mai-Phương Nguyễn, medicine woman, Vietnam War survivor, major depression and post-traumatic stress disorder survivor, Emmy Award–winning film and multimedia producer. Vietnam-born Mai-Phương shares the story of the family's departure from Vietnam aboard a United States helicopter following the war. Mai-Phương also shares about how stories and *Karuna* can heal and how she continues her work of advocacy in her community and beyond.

- Nnedi Ifudu Nweke, international trade lawyer and counsel at the leading international law firm Akin Gump Strauss Hauer & Feld LLP (Akin Gump). Raised in Nigeria, Nnedi shares her transition to the United States and how a single conversation with a fellow student at Harvard Law School shifted her mindset and helped her shed her self-doubt for good. She has rekindled that brilliance even through the most difficult tragedy of losing a young child.

- Linda Chey, CEO/Founder of BeMe Chic. Cambodia-born Linda shares her story of working in a Cambodian rice field at age three during the Vietnam War and living through three refugee camps. Linda seeks to live and share the childlike joy that was stolen by the war.

4.
True Healing Through *Karuna* and Storytelling

MAI-PHƯƠNG NGUYỄN, MD

Medicine Woman, Vietnam War Survivor, Major Depression and Post-Traumatic Stress Disorder Survivor, Emmy Award–Winning Film and Multimedia Producer

D r. Mai-Phương Nguyễn is a medicine woman who has survived three wars: (1) the Vietnam War, during which her family escaped Saigon as Communist tanks rolled into the South Vietnamese capital on April 29, 1975, when she was six years old; (2) the Los Angeles riots on April 29, 1992, when she was a third-year medical student at the University of Southern California; and (3) the ongoing war against her chronic major depression and post-traumatic stress disorder (PTSD) that was misdiagnosed and ineffectively treated for over twenty years.

After more than forty-five years of being displaced in America, Asia, and the Pacific Islands, now along with her young son, Mai-Phương has made her "home" in Little Saigon, Orange County, California. Little Saigon is home to the largest Vietnamese community outside of Vietnam.

Since 2011, Mai-Phương has built a viable solo private practice called Karuna Healthcare, Inc., serving vulnerable ethnic minority patients, the majority of whom have survived war and endured peace. Through innovation, she merges the latest telehealth technologies and up-to-date medical practices with tried and true traditional practices. Her mission is to be a healing agent for patients by empowering them to navigate the complex American healthcare system.

Another key pillar of her advocacy is to bring to light and de-stigmatize the impacts of war. She does these through her incredible, award-winning creations in film, television, and radio.

She is the associate producer of two landmark award-winning documentary films that tell the harrowing tales of Vietnamese boat people. Told through first-person narratives, both films were funded by PBS and screened nationwide on public television, as well as via international film festivals. Both reveal the displacements of generations of war survivors searching for freedom and "home" from a war that supposedly ended in 1975. *Bolinao 52* (2009) won two Emmy Awards and unearthed the unspeakable horrors of boat people, who endured cannibalism in their escape from Communist tyranny. *Stateless* (2013) tells of the enduring spirit of refugees stranded in the Philippines and how their journey to freedom in the West was made possible by decades of advocacy by refugee rights lawyers, who themselves were former child refugees.

Stateless won Audience Choice and Spotlight awards at the 2013 Vietnamese International Film Festival at the University of California, Irvine (UCI), where Mai-Phương completed her undergraduate studies decades earlier in 1991. During the height of the Vietnamese boat people crisis from 1987 to 1992, Mai-Phương learned how to use her voice and her pen to advocate for the resettlement and human rights of over two hundred thousand asylum-seeking refugees stranded in Southeast Asian refugee camps. At UCI, she served as the co-chairperson for a student organization called Project Ngoc (i.e., "Pearl").

From 2012 to 2014, Mai-Phương hosted a weekly Vietnamese radio program, *Sức Khỏe và Bạn* (*Health and You, Friend!*), on Vietnam

California Radio (VNCR) 106.3 FM, which reached over two hundred thousand Vietnamese listeners in the California southland. The impetus was to reach her ethnic community during the early years of the Affordable Care Act. She knew that Vietnamese Americans in Little Saigon (who fought against and fled a tyrannical Communist regime in post-1975 Vietnam) would be resistant to "state-mandated" health insurance. Despite not being fluent in her native-born Vietnamese language, *Sức Khỏe và Bạn* won the prestigious Excellence in Broadcast Journalism Award in 2013 from New American Media. In her forties, she endeavored to become more fluent in her mother tongue, in order to articulate trusted healthcare news to limited-English Vietnamese in the United States.

I MET MAI-PHƯƠNG in 2014 through our mutual book-writing coach. We were both aspiring nonfiction writers with the goal of sharing our immigrant experiences to help others navigate their journeys. We had a wonderful conversation about her travels to and within the United States since childhood as a refugee immigrant. Today, she is a patients' advocate and one of the most powerful and cogent voices of our time for victims of war and for healing from the invisible and intergenerational scars of war. She continues to break the tradition of "enduring and suffering in silence" that is imposed upon, and expected of, Asian women in general and Vietnamese immigrants in particular. She helps others find their path to authentic and enduring health by unraveling and honoring their life stories.

Twin Sounds
APRIL 29, 1975: STRAIGHT OUT OF SAIGON!

Six-year-old Mai-Phương and her family of six were evacuated from Saigon as part of the massive impromptu US military evacuation called Operation Frequent Wind. This makeshift mission was deployed by all the branches of the US military. Within the last days of the Vietnam War in late April 1975, over 120,000 Vietnamese people were evacuated out of Saigon. This evacuation was in response to what was recognized as an imminent victory of the Northern Vietnamese Communist insurgents. On the day before the city fell to the Communists, Mai-Phương's family was among the mobs of Vietnamese people storming the US Embassy and crowding onto overloaded helicopters and buses to escape a falling Saigon.

Her family was fortunate to escape Vietnam on April 29, 1975, because her father served as a translator for the press secretary to the president of South Vietnam. His job was to translate the news as it came across the teletype from Reuters or the Associated Press— from French and English into Vietnamese. As a side gig, her father also worked as the personal translator to his dear friend, Tony Paul, who at the time was the Pacific Rim Editor-in-Chief for *Reader's Digest*. It was Tony Paul who masterminded her family's complex exit out of Vietnam. As a career war correspondent who had reported on the contemporaneous collapse of nearby Cambodia in the weeks before South Vietnam's defeat at the end of April, Tony knew that the communists were advancing toward victory against the Americans.

In a vivid first memory of her childhood, Mai-Phương shared with me how Tony Paul assisted her family to defy traffic gridlock, pushing their way onto a school bus packed with frightened humans. They subsequently arrived at a secret rendezvous spot at Tan Son Nhat International Airport by dusk. Defying enemy fire, Tony Paul's large-framed Australian body and his true-grit courage helped to shepherd Mai-Phương, her parents, and her three siblings (ages three to eight) onto a US helicopter and out of harm's way. The overloaded helicopter delivered them onto the massive USS *Midway*, of the US Seventh Fleet, moored in the South China Sea. There they would be safe and protected by international laws honored by United Nations member countries.

While aboard the USS *Midway*, her father turned to her mother and reassured her that they were going to be safe. In less than twenty-four hours, while still aboard the USS *Midway*, around sunset on April 30, her family heard over the ship's intercom that the South Vietnamese national government had surrendered to the Northern Vietnamese Communist insurgents. It would herald the Fall of Saigon. It was the first of only two times in her entire life that she witnessed her childhood hero—her father—break down in tears. He cradled his head in his hands and sobbed in utter pain and sorrow. With red eyes, he looked up and lamented to his four young children and beautiful wife, "Our country is lost." Mai-Phương was still too young to fully understand the depth of her father's anguish. She would learn to live with that loss for most of her adult life.

For the next forty years, she would also learn to unpack and come to peace with that chaotic exodus out of her motherland. In her dreams and subconscious, that escape "straight out of Saigon" would haunt Mai-Phương again and again.

APRIL 29, 1992: BANG! BANG!

The Rodney King verdict had just been rendered, and the four white and Latino Los Angeles Police Department officers were found not guilty. As captured vividly on camera, the police officers had brutalized an unarmed Black man named Rodney King. In an angry response to the police brutality and systemic racism, mass riots broke out in Downtown and South Central Los Angeles. Violence, looting, gunfire, and destruction erupted in the streets. Throughout the "City of Angels," hell had broken loose. Meanwhile, twenty-three-year-old third-year medical student Mai-Phương was in lockdown, in her apartment in El Sereno (one of the poorest neighborhoods overlooking Downtown LA). While watching the KTLA Channel 5 evening news, she sat, paralyzed, listening to the hauntingly familiar sounds of chopper propellers overhead: *phuh-phuh-phuh-phuh!*

In the streets of Downtown LA below, gunshots were going off in all directions. Meanwhile, Mai-Phương watched the news footage of angry Black and brown men, women, and youth slashing tires, breaking windows, and setting mom-and-pop stores owned by Korean Americans on fire. Everywhere, people were yelling and screaming. As she watched in horror, she was unable to move. This was later diagnosed and labeled her first (of many) sentinel flashbacks that transported Mai-Phương straight back into her traumatic childhood exodus out of Saigon on April 29, 1975—exactly seventeen years earlier, to the day. The most traumatic day of her childhood was now linked to the most historical event of her young adulthood. It wasn't until over a dozen years later that a mental health specialist and counselor asked about and discovered this connection. That doctor was eighty-eight years old and was herself a war survivor of the Nazi occupation of her native Netherlands during World War II.

In the subsequent days, Mai-Phương had to report back to work in the emergency room of LA County's general hospital, LAC-USC, which is one of the largest public teaching hospitals in the United States. Here, on a daily basis, she saw large numbers of young Black and brown bodies come through, riddled with bullets. One particularly traumatic episode was when a sixteen-year-old Black boy lay on the operating table at 2:00 in the morning. Mai-Phương was the medical student whose job was to serve as the human retractor, to splay the abdomen wide open. Using all the force of her biceps and forearms for hours, she stood like a stoic robot as more-senior surgeons operated on both the gang member's chest and abdominal cavity, desperately seeking to find the sources of hemorrhage in his chest, while sewing up the bullet wounds in his bowels. Due to the profuse hemorrhage, the young boy experienced cardiac arrest. The surgeon screamed at a sleepy Mai-Phương to perform "cardiac massage." Years of medical training hadn't prepared her for this moment! He grabbed her gloved right hand and placed it directly on the youth's heart to pump it manually. Though she desperately tried to massage the nameless, dying, sixteen-year-old boy's heart back to life, she unfortunately failed to save him. It would take Mai-Phương decades to unpack and understand that traumatic experience of holding the bloodied heart of a teenager while he died in her helpless yet loving hands. In subsequent years, her desire to serve under-served communities would bring a retraumatizing, vicious cycle of bearing witness to poverty, social injustice, and violence.

Recycling of Trauma: The Life of a War-Child Turned Medicine Woman

Mai-Phương's PTSD battle took decades to diagnose because the Western medical model of healthcare missed the telltale signs and symptoms, again and again. Every few months or years, when she would fall into a mental health crisis and seek psychiatric care, the doctor would ask three screening questions: "Do you feel depressed?" "Do you feel hopeless?" "Do you feel so hopeless and depressed that you would want to end your life?" And if she answered yes to all three questions, the Western-trained psychiatrists would increase her current medication or switch to the newest drug of the day. In over fifteen years of seeking mental health care, she was never prescribed a medication that helped her. Rather, they caused debilitating side effects, including worsening anxiety, severe rashes, drowsiness, and a zombie-like numbness.

In hindsight, however, she realized that her refugee-childhood displacement, compounded by her "war-zone" medical training at LAC-USC, solidified her fears and anxieties of not being safe and never knowing enough to save the lives of those inequitably treated by society. When drug after antidepressant drug failed to cure her intermittent depressive episodes, Mai-Phương's depression was labeled by the psychiatrists as "refractory." Being labeled "refractory" in turn only reinforced her sense of hopelessness and helplessness.

The Asian American "Model Minority Myth" Exacerbates Mental Health Challenges

The chronic, intermittent major depression was also refractory in part because it was exacerbated by the Asian American Model Minority Myth. This is the myth that Asian Americans are expected to be "docile," stay quiet, keep their heads down, and assimilate. Culturally, Asian Americans are discouraged from speaking up and standing out. There was also the norm among first-generation Vietnamese refugee immigrants to "go along to get along." These were antithetical to Mai-Phương's fighting spirit and penchant for raising her voice in the face of injustice.

She also suffered from the survivor guilt that she was so much luckier than so many other poor, undereducated refugee immigrants. Unaware of this Model Minority Myth, from her first day in the United States, Mai-Phương has unconsciously held herself to impossibly high standards and expectations—imposed upon her by her parents and by American society. So much of this culturally piled-on pressure can be insidious.

These took a toll on her as a young adult and bled into her middle age, but she had no cognitive awareness of any underlying subliminal pressures. Mai-Phương (like so many high-achieving, first-generation refugee immigrants) was expected to always do right by her family, to "bring honor" and repay her parents for their intense sacrifices and to strive endlessly. These subconscious, toxic expectations (of Vietnamese and American cultural norms) set her up for automatic and incessant self-imposed "psychological warfare."

Mai-Phương spent almost three decades on a winding path to sustainable healing. This journey took her back to the island of Guam, where she returned as a licensed, board-certified doctor to care for Pacific Islanders and to face her own inner demons, far away from her parents and ethnic communities. It would also take her to Napa,

California, where she had a unique opportunity to own and run a solo private practice.

However, she fell in and out of bouts of major, crippling depression. Her most devastating episode was during the birth of her only son, at the advanced maternal age of forty-one in 2010. Thereafter, she endured postpartum depression and the stress of being a working mom, doctor, film producer, and wife to an aspiring filmmaker. All of these challenges forced her to reckon with and reflect on her seemingly "blessed and graced" herstory as one of the "luckier" Vietnamese refugees who left during the US evacuation out of Vietnam. It was not until she finally got properly diagnosed with PTSD (and not just major depression) that she was able to get culturally competent and trauma-informed mental health care.

Unfortunately, she would experience other unexpected challenges in subsequent years. When she finally let go of all the expectations of society (from both bicultural Vietnamese and American trappings) she tapped into her family's deep traditions of Buddhist practice that promote unattachment and mindfulness. This enabled Mai-Phương to fully sustain and remain in recovery from recurrent crippling depression by late 2018. The impetus for that transformation was a contentious and heartbreaking separation and divorce from her filmmaker husband and a protracted custody battle for her son.

The Union of Karuna and Western Healthcare

Mai-Phương's solo practice, Karuna Healthcare, Inc., specializes in house calls and telehealth consultations, with the aim of bringing back "the art of deep listening and compassionate, conscientious care." *Karuna* in ancient Sanskrit is the Buddhist concept of "unconditional compassion." For elders who suffer not only physical ailments, but also deep emotional, psychological, and spiritual wounds of war, the infusion of "deep, nonjudgmental listening" helps improve their overall wellness.

By redefining and reinventing her life's biography, in order to help heal a generation of elders from their unrecognized, undiagnosed, and unspoken traumatic physical, emotional, and moral injuries, Mai-Phương's work is extraordinary.

During the COVID-19 pandemic, Mai-Phương's visionary, high-touch, personalized healthcare practice could not have been more timely and urgent. The ability to see patients sheltered in place in their homes was highly effective in promoting their wellness. Whether patients live in cluttered and unkept single rooms for rent (a common scenario) or reside in multimillion-dollar homes in expensive neighborhoods (a rare and less common reality), Karuna Healthcare is impacting and improving health outcomes for elders who otherwise would get lost in the often disease-focused United States healthcare system. Through Karuna Healthcare, Mai-Phương Nguyễn combines Eastern practices with Zen Buddhist mindfulness listening, while incorporating state-of-the-art medicines and technologies to fight contagions like COVID-19 and addressing healthcare disparities created by systemic racism and classism.

Through her entrepreneurship, Mai-Phương has integrated her years of training and hard work—studying and apprenticing with the best clinicians in big cities like Los Angeles and Oakland, California, as well as remote communities like the Pueblo of Zuni, New Mexico, and rural Napa, California; remote islands like Guam and Saipan; and also developing communities in Tijuana, Mexico; Vellore, India; and war-ravaged Ninh Binh, Vietnam.

Mai-Phương is a weekly healthcare expert on Little Saigon TV (LSTV), which reaches a local and worldwide audience of the Vietnamese diaspora, including those living in Vietnam and abroad. Every Monday, she brings trusted breaking news about COVID-19 to her audience. Although the pandemic does not discriminate based on race and ethnicity, unfortunately, the media's tendencies to offer sensationalized news to garner more viewers at times propagates misinformation. To counter this, Mai-Phương dedicates hours to research in order to deliver trusted, science-based facts and information. Through her work in media, she is committed to continuing to equip the community to navigate the greatest healthcare challenges of the day, whatever they may be.

True Healing Through Art, Education, and Outreach

Today, Mai-Phương is part of a mental health movement in Southern California, through the nonprofit Viet-C.A.R.E. Their mission is revealed in the organization's acronym: Community Action Resource and Empowerment. Viet-C.A.R.E.'s challenge is to destigmatize the prevalent mental health challenges in the older generation of war survivors and to prevent the younger generation from suffering from the recycling of inherited, intergenerational traumas of war, displacement, and assimilation. Through collaborations with other mental health champions, Mai-Phương is able to uplift at-risk communities by using first-voice storytelling to conduct support groups and gatherings.

In the last few decades, she has helped to transform her own suffering, and that of her film subjects, her patients, and members of her communities, in order to heal their postwar trauma. This is the very definition of cultural and intergenerational competence and trauma-informed care. Through her life and work, she proves that the healing arts necessarily involve stories and that they are powerful. Mai-Phương's inspiring life and healing is captured in her motto: "In helping others heal, we help break the cycles of war and violence and transform the deep, painful wounds of war into lasting peace."

Mai-Phương's Definition of Success

For Mai-Phương, success is to live an authentic life—despite the deafening noise and expectations of others: "Whatever is your purpose and true joy, find it, chase it, and live it. Honor your familial traditions (the good parts that nurture your sense of self and worth), but listen to your true heart, and do not get distracted by the ethereal and superficial metrics of 'success.'" To Mai-Phương, success is having the freedom to chase her life's passions and to be free from the norms and expectations of the outside world that may never understand or validate her.

MAI-PHƯƠNG'S IMMIGRACE

- Medicine woman and patients' advocate
- Story-collector and healer
- Multimedia (TV, radio, social media) producer who empowers through storytelling

MAI-PHƯƠNG'S IMMIGEMS

◇ *Be culturally sensitive and linguistically competent.* Understanding one's herstory is the key to unlocking and understanding one's roots, which one needs to do in order to map out one's destiny. It's important to embrace and unpack our complex herstory, so that we can overcome our past adversities. When we *own* our traumas, and face them, they no longer haunt or harm us.

◇ *Understand that violence begets violence.* In order to break the cycle of violence, to thrive, and to truly be free, we must begin to speak unspeakable truths about the immense violence of war and all forms of violence, be they in thoughts, words, actions, representation, policies, or lack thereof.

◈ *Believe that together, we can make a difference.* It matters that you care about things outside of your comfort zone, and when you get together with people who are equally or even more passionate, together you can make a difference. Together, we can be the change.

5.
Own Your Brilliance

NNEDI IFUDU NWEKE
Preeminent International Trade Lawyer and Expert

Nnedi Ifudu Nweke is a partner and an international trade lawyer at the leading law firm Akin Gump Strauss Hauer & Feld LLP. She obtained her Bachelor of Arts in economics and political science from the University of Connecticut and her Juris Doctor (JD) from Harvard Law School.

Following law school, she was an associate at Norton Rose Fulbright, and she was previously an associate and senior counsel at Akin Gump.

Nnedi is a leading international legal expert, and she counsels global clients on US laws and policy affecting cross-border transactions, including export control laws, economic sanctions and trade embargoes, and anti-corruption laws, including the US Foreign Corrupt Practices Act and anti–money laundering laws.

Nnedi represents clients in trade matters before US government departments and agencies, including the Departments of Commerce, State, and the Treasury. She has helped clients in various industries to effectively manage due-diligence investigations in connection with investment-fund formation, mergers, acquisitions, and other transactions.

Nnedi advises clients on how to respond to US government investigations, develop and implement compliance policies and procedures, prepare voluntary self-disclosures, and conduct internal reviews, audits, and investigations. Her practice extends to drafting license applications, delisting petitions, advisory opinion requests, and other submissions to relevant US government agencies.

As a preeminent expert in the fields of international trade law and business, Nnedi speaks frequently at conferences and on podcasts, and she has been quoted in industry journals, providing subject matter expertise and counsel.

Nnedi is a recipient of the 2021 Minority Corporate Counsel Association Rising Star award and the 2018 *National Law Journal*'s D.C. Rising Star award, and was part of the Transaction Team of the Year, who received recognition for their pro bono work on human rights in Iran.

AS THE ONLY two Nigerians in Harvard Law School's JD class of 2003, Nnedi and I were destined to meet. By the time the first semester rolled around, mutual friends and family had mentioned her name to me, and vice versa, so we made sure to find each other. We became roommates in our second and third years of law school and are forever friends.

Shedding the Burden of Self-Doubt

A casual conversation with a classmate during Nnedi's second year of law school led to a powerful mindset shift.

You see, throughout the first year of law school, Nnedi had carried this burden of self-doubt. The first year of law school, known in law schools as 1L year, is intense. The curriculum is rigorous and is unlike anything students encountered in college.

Nnedi went, as 1Ls at Harvard Law School do, from being one of the smartest kids in college to being at a school where everyone is brilliant. Nnedi looked around and thought, *Everyone is smarter than I am. I most certainly don't belong here.* So she carried that burden of self-doubt throughout the first year of law school. But, relying on what she knew had brought her that far, she spent long hours at Harvard's Langdell law library, often from when the doors were opened in the morning till they were closed for the night. When she was not in class or grabbing a quick meal, you could bet money you would find Nnedi at Langdell.

Nnedi was pleasantly surprised to receive excellent grades after the first year of law school. When she returned for the first semester of 2L year, she was having a casual conversation with an American-born Jewish friend and classmate when he surprised Nnedi by sharing his grade from the contracts course they took together. She had received a better grade than he did! Nnedi realized that she deserved to be at Harvard Law School.

She's eternally grateful to that classmate because he unwittingly taught her in that moment that if you work hard and do your very best, you will do great things and exceed your own expectations. And so she shed that heavy burden of self-doubt.

A Storrs Tradition

Nnedi was born in the United States, but she returned to Nigeria as an infant. Unlike most of her peers in Nigeria, she attended a day school, rather than attending boarding school for middle and high schools. She returned to the United States in 1996 to attend college at the University of Connecticut (UConn) in Storrs, Connecticut.

Both of Nnedi's parents also attended UConn—they were engaged when they arrived from Nigeria to Storrs, where they eventually married. They had a longstanding desire for their three children (of which Nnedi is the middle child) to receive the terrific education they did. Her brother, Eloka, led the way, and Nnedi subsequently joined him.

It was her first time away from her parents for an extended period of time. Without the security of her parents, Nnedi felt both anxiety and excitement, but mostly anxiety. It was somewhat helpful that Eloka was already there. She spent most of her school breaks in Boston, where her aunt lived, but she rotated through the homes of other aunts and uncles in Indiana and New York.

Nnedi is highly self-aware and self-motivated, so she had no trouble pushing herself to study hard and excel academically. She sat in front of every class and took meticulous notes.

Perhaps her greatest adjustment to the United States was outside of the classroom—going from being well-known and popular (not what you would call a party girl, but certainly the belle of the ball in high school in Nigeria) to being just one of the other girls in college. She had left her entire social network behind, including all her friends.

In spite of having her brother around, she felt like a fish out of water, with all the self-doubt most teenage girls experience. *Am I pretty enough? Am I good enough?* It also made her realize that she was not as open-minded as she may have initially thought. She was surprised at her own reserve and that she didn't make friends as easily as her brother, the quintessential "man of the people."

Three things made her transition possible and helped her to come into her own by her junior and senior years of college. The first was having her brother and his established circle of friends. The second was joining the gospel choir. (She had heard it was a fun class. She made friends in the comfort of that group, including the woman who became her best friend, an immigrant from Barbados, who shared and understood the immigrant experience.) The third was that Nnedi relied on her faith. The Catholic mass is the same in Lagos, Nigeria, as it is in Storrs, Connecticut. When she made time to pray in the chapel or attended mass, she could close her eyes and just as easily picture herself in a chapel in Lagos. The chapel was serene and tranquil. It was home.

Greater Heights

Nnedi initially set her sights on Georgetown Law. One of her college friends, who likely saw her incredible drive, determination, and sheer smarts, encouraged her to apply to Harvard Law School. Once this seed was planted in Nnedi, there was no looking back. She didn't doubt her ability to get into Harvard. One of her close cousins had attended the Harvard School of Public Health, so there was precedent, leading to family support and encouragement of her goal. She applied to several law schools—safe schools, reach schools, and dream schools. She remembered receiving offers and generous financial aid packages from several lower-ranked schools but not feeling excited at all. She waited for Harvard till she received her acceptance letter. She was elated.

The Time Is Now

Making partner at a law firm wasn't initially a goal for Nnedi. After graduating from law school, Nnedi began her legal career as an associate at Norton Rose Fulbright. She subsequently joined Akin Gump as an associate. She then spent two years as counsel and another two years as senior counsel.

Opting for the counsel track meant she was on a modified schedule and was expected to put in 80 percent of the time. Law firm billable hours are typically over two thousand hours a year, so 80 percent was no measly time investment, either.

2018 was a year of mindset shifts for Nnedi. It would mark her fortieth birthday and her tenth year at Akin Gump. Something about milestones make us take stock of where we are and where we are going.

The biggest catalyst that led Nnedi to consider partnership was when a partner told her during her year-end conversation that it was time for her to start thinking about her business plan for partnership. Something clicked. This recommendation was from someone who'd given her tough feedback in the past. One of her mentors had previously told her to consider partnership, but she may have discounted this advice since he was in her corner. Hearing this from someone who'd previously provided tough feedback registered differently for her because she knew he wasn't paying her lip service.

This, combined with her receiving outreach from recruiters and companies seeking out attorneys to fill in-house counsel roles, caused her to begin to reflect on where she was and where she wanted to go. She loved her firm, the people, and what she was doing.

While a number of private companies had approached her, they didn't approach her with work that excited her—doing international work, and doing it with people she loves.

So she asked herself a couple of powerful questions: *Why not keep doing this? And why not elevate my voice?* She wanted to feel like she had more of a stake in this thing in which she was investing so much of her time.

Simultaneously, a lot was happening in 2018. It was the height of US sanctions against Russia and Russian oligarchs. Nnedi's work at the firm was highly visible and getting a lot of attention. There was a natural buzz about her and what she did. One thing was clear to her: the time was now.

Convincing her practice leaders of this wasn't easy. People were skeptical. In a certain sense, in opting for the counsel track, she had taken herself out of the partnership equation. She had to undertake a campaign to convince people that she really wanted this, and that she would hustle, do the work, and bring in clients, rather than being a service partner, who relied on other partners to bring in clients. The metrics and numbers needed to add up in order to get the practice leaders and partnership admissions committee on board with the idea.

As she went through the rigorous "campaign" process, at some point someone suggested that she wait until the following year, in order to put up the strongest possible case. Intuitively, Nnedi was convinced that 2018 was the year. Her response to the idea of waiting a year was therefore a firm, "No, the time is now."

The next step in the multistep process was getting the practice leaders to nominate her. She'd made her case to them, and she was on vacation in Bermuda with her family when she received the call that she'd been put up for partner. She subsequently interviewed and met with representatives of the partnership admissions committee. Then it was out of her hands, and the committee went to work.

In October, Nnedi went on a girlfriends' trip to Mexico in anticipation of her fortieth birthday. She was on the beach when her practice leader called and delivered the wonderful birthday news. The partnership committee approved her admission as partner.

Strong Relationships Are Rocket Fuel

Over the course of her career, Nnedi developed a depth of expertise in sanctions, anti-corruption, and anti–money laundering laws that few attorneys attain. Based on work she'd managed in connection with the Ukraine/Russia sanctions regime, and with the imposition of increased US sanctions against various individuals and entities in Russia in 2018, her work became invaluable in helping clients navigate doing business in various territories. She took the helm in assisting severely affected clients and managing the most challenging engagements on behalf of the firm.

In sharing advice to law firm associates who hope to become partner, Nnedi emphasizes the power of networks. In an interview with the *American Lawyer* for a Q and A column, titled "How I Made Partner," Nnedi notes: "The road to partnership is about much more than doing excellent legal work. Get out of your office and network within the firm. Meaningful relationships are invaluable."[1]

Nnedi had no immediate models in her family for what it means to be a partner at an international law firm. Growing up in Nigeria in an academically strong family, she believed in her potential and was taught that she could do anything. In the United States, however, immigrants are not in entirely familiar territory, and while Nnedi doesn't fully embrace the idea of being an outsider, it is not the case that immigrants are unaffected by growing up in different cultures and contexts. Nnedi believes there is something to be said about windows. It's one thing to have someone open doors for you, but it is also great to see your reflection. Those who have similar experiences to us can be those windows, in which we can see powerful reflections of what is possible for us.

Finding Healthy Resilience

Tragedy destabilized Nnedi when her twenty-month-old son, Izu, passed away.

In the darkest days and months that followed, Nnedi felt shock, grief, anger, and a variety of painful emotions. Most of the time, she felt like she was floating. It was unlike any experience she'd encountered in the past—the loneliness of adjusting to a new environment and country in college and the challenges of being a junior associate at a large law firm all paled in comparison. This pain was deep and unfathomable, even indescribable. The tools that had anchored her in moments of trial in the past didn't help at all.

A few things did help Nnedi process this tragic experience. The first was therapy. Nnedi and her husband saw a therapist regularly for over a year and occasionally thereafter. It was helpful to speak to someone about how they were feeling and to check in on how the tools were helping them. She came to understand and appreciate the differences in the ways she and her husband grieved.

Some prefer to talk to priests, but for Nnedi, particularly given the anger she felt (including anger toward God that this happened), therapy was most helpful in processing the painful emotions. She found her way back to her faith because after a while, she felt rudderless, and faith provided an anchor and a sense of being rooted in something greater.

The second thing that helped was work. Nnedi didn't want to return to work too soon, but getting back into the routine and applying herself at work was a helpful distraction.

The final thing was resiliency. For better or worse, and for as long as she lives, Nnedi will find a way and will keep going. As immigrants, we have that resilient spirit to persevere, but it is important not to persevere without help. Part of healthy resilience is getting help. Set stigma aside, and get the help you need.

There were, of course, the close Nigerian relatives who thought she went to therapy for far too long. "Isn't it enough?" they asked, in a tone that Nigerians would recognize from their older relatives. "Enough for whom?" Nnedi asked. Only she could declare that she'd received enough of the support she needed. You have to live your life on your own terms. Several aspects of our cultural thinking, including the views of relatives, are well-intentioned, but it is important to know when to set aside certain aspects of culture for your own well-being.

Grieving is not time barred. There is no deadline or finish line. When you lose a child tragically, the healing journey is lifelong. The pain may dull, but the ache will always be there.

One of the things Nnedi took away from this experience was valuing time with family. Her definition of success is grounded in a knowing that family time is a gift and privilege.

Nnedi's Definition of Success

"What is success?" is a question Nnedi asks herself often because the race doesn't end. Once you climb one mountain, there's another hill, so she frequently reflects on what success means to her. She says, "I want to spend time with my husband and my two children. I want to be happy. I want to travel. Success is living in this space where there is, on average, an equilibrium between work and home. We know there are times when work will dominate. And other times when work will give way to family priorities and commitments. If I'm able to do work I enjoy, and I'm available to my family and they are not feeling the deficit, then I feel successful."

A lot of lawyers are successful in terms of the amount of compensation they command. Although money is one metric of success, Nnedi is not singularly motivated by money. She elevates the things that make her happy and healthy, and she includes herself and her self-care in that definition of family time—exercising, caring for her mental health, and also helping children with homework and being present at children's events (even if not all of them).

Nnedi is conscious that she's the woman in her home. She outsources what she can, such as housekeeping and occasionally catering meals for the family, while reserving the right to roll up her sleeves and whip up some *onugbu* soup. She also recognizes that certain things, such as being a wife, mother, and taking care of her mental health, cannot be outsourced, so she sees to it that the things that are important to her are taken care of and that she's creating a happy life, as she defines it.

NNEDI'S IMMIGRACE

- Preeminent international trade lawyer and expert

NNEDI'S IMMIGEMS

◇ *Master soft skills; hard work won't take you all the way.* The immigrant experience is not monolithic, but one could make the following generalization: most immigrants come from backgrounds where hard work is ingrained. Immigrants are raised to believe that you can achieve whatever you want as long as you work hard. If you work hard, things will work out. This idea is rooted in meritocracy. Meritocracy will get you far, and hard work is indeed rewarded. But hard work and meritocracy won't take you all the way. As immigrants, we should also pay attention to soft skills. What has gotten Nnedi to where she is aren't just the principles she studied at the Langdell law library. If you're not socially intelligent and don't know how to influence, navigate, read a room, network, be malleable and adaptable, and know when to bend, you will only go so far.

◇ *Be authentically you, because being a caricature is tedious.* It is okay to be authentically who you are. A lot of immigrants go to great lengths to fit into American society. Some shed their names and other aspects of their identities. The problem is that people can sniff out counterfeits. They can sense when we are not being ourselves. This is different from code-switching and being adaptable. Don't lose yourself in the process of integration, and don't create a huge gulf between who you are at work and who you are outside of work. Be professional in your work, but bring your full Nigerian American, Russian American, or Argentinean American self. It is okay if not all your words sound American and if people occasionally ask for clarification on your words. Own it. Being yourself will be easier. If you are a caricature, it's tedious. There's something impenetrable about caricatures. They create a gulf. And if people can't penetrate, they feel like they don't know and can't trust, advocate for, fully connect, or align with you.

◇ *Connect with your purpose.* The key to Nnedi's longevity in her career is being able to connect with her defined purpose. Not everybody is fortunate enough to marry their job with their purpose. Nnedi has, and she is grateful for this. There are two kinds of Africans in the diaspora: There are those who come to the United States, or elsewhere in the developed world, obtain education or experience, and return to their home countries to build. This is admirable. And then there are those who, while they remain abroad, stay connected to their homeland and find bridges to continue to develop their home countries. Nnedi is in the second category. She advises US and non-US companies seeking to invest in sub-Saharan Africa. She provides guidance on navigating corruption and other ills. She believes that strategic partnerships are key to continually developing Africa, and, through her work, she enables investors to contribute to building a more prosperous Africa.

6.
Childlike Joy

LINDA CHEY
Entrepreneur and Chief Executive Officer of BeMe Chic

Linda Chey is the CEO, founder, and owner of BeMe Chic, which provides clothing and accessories for men and women as well as consulting services. Linda has two college degrees, in marketing and international business, from California State University, Long Beach. She supports various causes in Cambodia, but has never returned home.

SPEAKING ABOUT HER childhood with me brought back cogent memories (and tears) for Linda. Yet she spoke with such warmth and passion about her journey from war and isolation to living a life of sales and service.

Run for Your Life!

Linda ran amid other children under age ten, who, like her, had spent much of the previous three years working in Cambodian rice fields surrounded by killing fields and genocide.

Their collective cry was urgent, and they pranced like their lives depended on it. The war was over. It was about twelve-thirty in the afternoon on April 30, 1975. Linda ran to her grandmother's house. Her family was reunited. Linda's aunts, uncles, and cousins all returned. But Linda had lost her birth father in the war.

Beyond the relief that the battle guns had been silenced, one thing became certain: it was time to leave Cambodia, which was now under the Communist Khmer Rouge. The Khmer Rouge was a brutal regime that ruled Cambodia under the leadership of Marxist dictator Pol Pot. The Khmer Rouge was responsible for the deaths of more than two million people. The regime's tactics included social engineering and the capture and murder of intellectuals, the wealthy, and others who were considered to be threats to the regime. In addition to murder and killing fields, people also died from overworking, disease, malnutrition, or starvation.

Beginning in the 1960s, the Khmer Rouge had operated as an armed wing of the Communist Party of Kampuchea in Cambodia. In 1970, a military coup overthrew the then-ruling monarch, Prince Norodom Sihanouk, who then formed a coalition with the Khmer Rouge. Between 1970 and 1975, civil war raged between the supporters of the Prince Norodom and Khmer Rouge alliance and the right-leaning military that was responsible for the coup.

In 1975, the Khmer Rouge took over the capital city of Phnom Penh, thereby winning the civil war. Rather than reinstating Prince Norodom, they handed power to Pol Pot, the leader of the Khmer Rouge.

With the Khmer Rouge in power, there was much uncertainty, and circumstances could change at any time. Linda's family wanted a better life. They wanted safety. They wanted security. They wanted freedom.

But none of those came quickly. First, they had to pass through a crucible.

War, Separation, and Jungle Life

Linda's childhood memories are vivid and palpable. Recounting them awoke painful emotions.

She was forced into child labor in rice fields at age four. She was separated from her parents and siblings. Life on the rice fields was a jungle and a living hell. Linda cried every night, but she observed, "The interesting thing about living under such conditions is that you remember when things were better. Not perfect, but better. The human spirit rejects being dehumanized."

One of the Khmer Rouge's wartime strategies was separation from family. Linda's mother, Bory Keo, had been forcibly taken away to an unknown location. The child laborers lived in the jungle with no parents, siblings, or relatives.

To reinforce the separation, adult family members weren't allowed to visit the children on the rice fields, but the children were sent to visit family once every three months. Linda's closest relative at the time was her grandmother. Linda walked two to three hours—on bare feet, rain or shine—to take advantage of the golden opportunity to see Grandma. Linda's grandfather was good with crops, so the Khmer Rouge let him live. Linda fully embraces her Cambodian roots. Her grandparents had roots in China. They immigrated to Cambodia in 1942, during World War II, and met in Cambodia.

The children lived in shelters that stood approximately nine feet off the ground. They slept on three-by-four-foot wood allotments. They had no beds, sheets, duvets, or pillows. There were no bathrooms either. Children who dared to venture outside at night were attacked by wolves and other wild animals, or they feared they would be, since it had happened on several occasions. So their "beds" also became their bathrooms. The realization that one needed to use the bathroom was accompanied by immense dread—dread at the thought of venturing into the dark, dangerous woods, and dread at the discomfort one was about to create. Their living quarters reeked.

At sunrise, the children set about their work in the rice fields. At around 12:30 p.m., they ate their meager lunch, which was just enough to keep them alive and no more. Rice soup it was, day in and day out. The rice was mixed with a little bit of vegetables and salt. It was bland and hardly a nutritious meal, but the children gobbled it up. During their infrequent visits, Linda's grandma advised her to eat quickly because if she didn't, someone else would take her meal. It was survival of the fittest. This was jungle life. Linda still eats quickly today.

Living in the jungle without family, in the midst of a war, and with death and destruction all around her, she experienced fear, famine, disease, and malnutrition. Linda came close to death three times. She experienced high fevers, along with tremors and blurred vision. But no one was there to take care of her and nurse her back to health. Infancy to age five are the most critical years of a child's development—these are particularly vulnerable years, when the body develops its immunity. A good chunk of those years were stolen from Linda.

A Sense of Helplessness

During the civil war and subsequently with the Khmer Rouge in power, there was a sense of helplessness in Cambodia. Linda's biological father tried to escape three times. The first time, he tried to escape with Linda and her sister and join members of his immediate family who had escaped to Vietnam. He subsequently tried two more times to escape. Escape was a dangerous option. Being captured by the Khmer Rouge during an attempted escape meant death. The Khmer Rouge viewed escape as betrayal to the country, which made one an "enemy of the state."

When the war was over, the family put out advertising to look for him in neighboring towns and villages.

When the family escaped to Thailand in 1980, Bory Keo continued putting out ads to let Linda's father know that the family had survived. They never received responses from him. The family believed that, had he survived, he would have seen the ads. After years of looking for him, they gave up. When the family eventually saw his relatives in Cambodia, the relatives said Linda's father didn't survive. Bory Keo had also seen in a dream that he had been captured and executed.

Before Liberation

With the end of the war and the decision to leave Cambodia, a new chapter in Linda's childhood hell began. The family left Cambodia in hopes of starting a new life in the United States. Bory Keo took Linda and three other children (ages six, eight, and ten) to another province to pick up their aunt, uncle, and three cousins, and the group walked for two weeks, crossing the border to Thailand, where they lived in a refugee camp. Linda was about eight years old at the time.

Linda's mom had remarried, but the war's impact on her stepfather, John Chey, was immense. He, too, felt helpless, dejected, and depressed that they had left Cambodia but were unable to reach the United States. To further complicate matters, he was accused of being a spy. Unable to cope, he ran away. Bory Keo hired a messenger, who eventually found and returned him to the family.

Linda's family lived in four overcrowded refugee camps, where disease and malnutrition ran rampant. Women experienced additional layers of trauma, such as widespread rape and abortion and systemic discrimination. As a married woman, Bory Keo's securing of refugee status also was delayed because it was on the condition of having a husband who could take care of her.

After a failed attempt to obtain passes through the Canadian embassy, the family spent close to five years in four different refugee camps in Thailand and six months in the Philippines.

The ten family members finally made it to the United States in 1985, ten years after the end of the war.

Instant Entrepreneurs

Something about the United States inspires and supports entrepreneurship. As soon as the family arrived in California, they began to collect recyclable cans and exchange them for cash. They would wake up, bright and early, at 5:30 a.m., collect cans, and then hop on the school bus. Their Datsun pickup truck had to beat the garbage trucks. They also bought vegetables and sold them out of their Datsun. If Linda's father could work twenty-four hours every day, he would. While Linda and her siblings were at school, their mom would stay home and sew, earning about fifty cents per garment.

Although those early days in the United States were rough, as Linda recounted this chapter of her story, a different, joyful mood emerged.

They obtained their daily needs from factory castaways. Linda sounded almost giddy when describing their adventures in factory disposal bins. They'd go to the warehouse, sometimes while factory workers tossed goods into large bins. Linda, with her siblings, mom, and stepfather, would stand in the bins and collect items, dodging incoming cans. This accounted for canned foods, rice, detergent, bathing soap, chocolate, Snickers, and Butterfingers. Linda loved this part!

They got their clothes this way too. They picked up clothes that had been thrown out, then laundered them for their own use. On rare occasions, they bought used clothes by the pound, for about a dollar. Kmart and Target were completely beyond reach.

What they didn't use or consume, they repackaged and sold in poor neighborhoods. Linda's parents were an ambitious pair, and within a year of living in the United States, they opened a business. Every year thereafter, they launched a new business, ranging from grocery and ninety-nine cent stores to painting and flooring companies.

Discovering Her Passion

The family settled in Long Beach, California, home to the largest population of Cambodians outside of Cambodia. At age fifteen, Linda was a multilingual—she spoke Cambodian, Chinese, English, and Spanish—entrepreneurial teen. Bory Keo was no "tiger mother."[1] Linda and her mom bonded over check cashing and coordinating butchering duties. Linda ran the meat department at their grocery store, sometimes skipping school to work.

Over time, Linda's parents were involved in multiple businesses. Linda's mother was a saver, and this enabled the family to quickly purchase businesses and reinvest. Linda learned frugality from her mother. They owned a liquor store and a discount store, and they also invested in real estate. They continually bought and reinvested in businesses. At some point, the family had three or four businesses.

Linda thrived as a salesperson, selling to customers of all nationalities. Whoever walked through the door, she likely spoke their language and thus would connect with them. Teenage Linda didn't spend any time hanging out with friends or clubbing, but she didn't seem to regret missing out on the typical adolescent experience, unlike her lost childhood. As the one who showed up at school looking greasy and bearing a combination of food aromas, she was happy to trade business for education. Those years helped Linda discover her passion for sales.

Today, Linda owns a successful business in Long Beach, California. BeMe Chic was initially founded as a 600-square-foot venture, before growing and reopening at a larger location on Anaheim Street. The store features elegant clothing and accessories for women and men, as well as consulting services. A full-service hair salon is also available on-site. During the COVID-19 pandemic, Linda launched her own clothing line.

Because Linda lost much of her childhood on the rice fields and in refugee camps, she cherishes time with her children and seeks to relive her own childhood through their experiences and the joys she's able to provide for them in the United States.

From a childhood on rice fields in the midst of the Khmer Rouge and genocide—and from picking clothes out of dumpsters to launching, sustaining, and growing her own successful clothing boutique—Linda continues to seek out and live her childlike joy. She also believes in growing from one's experiences: "You don't want to live in the past," she says. "You need to grow out of it."

Linda's Definition of Success

For Linda, success includes hard work, great work ethic, and generosity What you put into life and business, you eventually receive in return; so put in solid business principles, ethics, and morals.

Be generous with those around you. Give back, without expectation, to communities—churches, schools, and other charitable causes.

Believe in balance. Success is not limited to working hard at one's profession, but includes spending quality time with family.

LINDA'S IMMIGRACE

- Gifted Fashion Entrepreneur and Saleswoman

LINDA'S IMMIGEMS

- ◇ *Always put yourself in others' shoes.* Being a passionate marketer, Linda believes clients' needs are paramount. Always tune in, listen, and truly understand what your clients want.

- ◇ *Be a person of integrity.* With employees, vendors, clients, and all stakeholders, always treat people with respect.

- ◇ *Believe in balance.* It may not happen in the first two or three years of business, but you only have one life to live, so make a commitment to find balance.

Immigrace Journal

BRILLIANCE BLUEPRINT #2
Inner Self-Mastery: *Find Joy*

1. What are the top three negative experiences of my life?

    _____
    _____
    _____

2. What did I learn from those experiences?

    _____
    _____
    _____

3. Why can I be grateful for them?

    _____
    _____
    _____

4. How will I continue to support myself to grow through them?

    _____
    _____
    _____

5. Who has the expertise to support me to grow through them? (Choose wisely. Various circumstances will require different sorts of expertise. For example, grief, depression, marriage/family, and business challenges call for radically different skill sets. Choose experts who have attained the results you seek, either for themselves or for other clients. Resist the temptation to conflate success, e.g., taking marriage advice from a celebrity who may have attained success as a movie star, but who hasn't attained the results you'd like to see in your own marriage.)

_____
_____
_____

6. How will I nourish my faith and spiritual life?

a. Daily _____

b. Weekly _____

c. Monthly _____

d. Yearly _____

7. How will I find my joy every day?

_____
_____
_____

8. Three things that bring me joy:

_____
_____
_____

9. True joy is:

_____

_____

_____

10. True fulfillment is:

_____

_____

_____

11. I'm joyful when:

_____

_____

_____

12. I'll contribute to my joy every day by:

_____

_____

_____

13. Emotion is energy in motion. We can gain mastery of our emotions by recognizing and acknowledging them and by understanding them as things we do and engage in (as opposed to things that happen to us).

   a. Three positive emotions I regularly engage in are:

   _____

   _____

   _____

   b. Three negative emotions I regularly engage in are:

   _____

   _____

   _____

14. I'll manage my emotions by:

_____

_____

_____

15. What are my values?

_____

_____

_____

(I'm astounded by how few adults actually know what they value and do not. Part of owning your journey is owning your place in the world and the things that drive you. It's been said that individuals are often motivated by increasing pleasure and avoiding pain. Values are emotional states that we believe are important to experience or avoid.

Our values can change over time, but lack of awareness is a true immigrace killer. If you don't know what you value, you are guaranteeing that you will not live your purpose in life, that you will likely be unhappy, and that you'll advance others' values.

Examples of values we move toward: joy, freedom, peace, adventure, success, love, trust, courage, empathy, growth, faith, passion, security, achievement, compassion.

Examples of values we avoid: sadness, sorrow, failure, rejection, anger, loneliness, depression, boredom, apathy, guilt, helplessness, frustration.)

PART III
Dare to Play in the Big Leagues
Set and Accomplish Big Goals

"Immigrants, due to our accents, are better suited for technical work or crunching numbers—accounting, engineering, and other technical stuff. We don't make great lawyers."

I've characterized this as some of the worst career advice I ever received. It came from an uncle who'd recommended my sister and me for part-time jobs at a bank in New York City while we were in college. We'd been in the United States for less than two years. He'd lived in the United States for close to two decades, and in the spirit of sharing well-meaning uncle advice, he had asked about our professional aspirations. I dared to tell him I wanted to be a lawyer.

Over the years—well after I obtained a Juris Doctor from Harvard Law School and began to practice law—as I've considered why I ignored his advice, it boils down to one thing: belief. I believed I could accomplish what I desired, so I continued in the direction of my goal.

Once you've said yes to your immigrace and committed to doing the inner work, you must set and accomplish big goals.

The Importance of Intention and Goal Setting

Intention and goal setting are about managing your focus. They are the vehicles that will carry you to the destinations you want to go and help you realize your legacy. Intentions are broader and non-specific desires that we'd love to realize. Goals are more specific and action-oriented.

Massive goals and intentions tend to elicit a lot of negative "what-ifs." What if they don't happen? What if I fail? What will people say? What if I look stupid? What if they're too unrealistic? What if I don't know how? What if I encounter obstacles? What if I have to change them? What if it's the wrong goal?

First, you can ask better what-ifs: What if they support me in living out my immigrace? What if they support me in being happier? What if they help me to be love in the world? What if they help me bring more happiness to those around me?

The great news about big goals is that they are journeys. They are not completed in a single step. They take you on highways, byways, streams, and rivers and through valleys and seasons—fall, winter, spring, and summer. The twists, turns, and conclusions are not obvious. If you are one who values certainty more highly than adventure or uncertainty, yes, big goals will scare you.

One illustration of the execution of a long-term goal is this book. This book took me over seven years to write. If I had known at the beginning of the process that it would take this long, the impatient side of me would've said, *No, let's find something we can accomplish much more quickly!* Yet, I knew this goal was rooted in something deeper. It was something that was critical for me to accomplish in order to serve the world. I knew it was a worthwhile journey.

In our current age, and with the prevalence of various publishing options, books can be brought into the world at staggering speed. My impatient side found the idea of speed compelling. But there remained the side that acknowledged that certain creative projects take longer to bring into fruition. Indeed, some of the greatest creative projects in history took long periods of time.

If you set a massive goal, be patient with yourself and with the process of realizing it. Faster is not always better. Better is better. And sometimes better takes longer. Yet, we must also maintain a sense of urgency that propels us to take massive action. This enables us to make steady progress toward the long-term goals and improves learning along the way.

You Are At War With Your Legacy And You Don't Even Know It

I've often said that a lot of us are at war with our legacies and don't even know it.

First, it is worth understanding what legacy is. Legacy is how you want your life to be summarized at the end of it, how you want to be remembered, or what you want your life to stand for. Sadly, most leaders don't take the time to reflect on what they want their entire existence on earth to stand for. This is why most of us stumble through life, feel like we are on a hamster wheel, and feel like we lack direction. It is important to define your intended legacy because it helps give your life purpose and meaning, and can serve as a compass. You can continually return to it in order to determine whether you are headed in your intended direction. Fortunately or unfortunately, no one can define it for you. You have to put in the time to consider, define, and commit to it. I'm an enormous proponent of not just leaving a legacy behind, as most people often think about the term, but of *living* it every day.

If you disagree that you are at war with your legacy, consider some of the most common weapons you may use to wage war on your legacy:

- By failing to define it
- By failing to prioritize it
- By ignoring it
- By being fearful
- By hesitating
- By procrastinating
- By staying in your comfort zone
- By failing to live it

The biggest life and career risk is to fail to evaluate both from the perspective of legacy. The outcome is immense pain, regret, frustration, and lack of fulfillment.

The legacy I hope to live is closely related to my definition of success, which is included later in the book. It is less about what I'm doing, but about who I'm being. I hope to be a positive force in this world and to be an example of love, joy, and human potential. And then there are big things I hope to accomplish, which include helping immigrant women realize their potential, and helping move Nigeria, Africa, and the developing world to the realization of their fullest potential.

A non-exhaustive list of questions to help you get started on defining your legacy is included in this section's Immigrace Journal.

Habits Define Your Legacy

John Maxwell (through whom I was first introduced to the idea of legacy as a leadership principle in his *21 Irrefutable Laws of Leadership* book) famously said that "You'll never change your life until you change something you do daily," and "the secret of your success is found in your daily habits."[1] While legacy is a life-defining word, it is built on micro-moments and micro-decisions throughout the day.

Habits have the power to define our lives. In his book *The Power of Habit*, Charles Duhigg describes habits as a formula your brain automatically follows. According to a 2006 Duke University study cited in Duhigg's book, more than 40 percent of the actions people perform each day aren't due to decision-making, but are habits. As our brains get accustomed to performing a particular activity, less conscious decision-making is involved. The activity becomes automatic and virtually unconscious.[2]

We gain greater mastery of our lives when we examine those unconscious activities and ensure that they support our goals and who we want to be in the world. The first step in mastering our habits is awareness. A great practice is to audit your habits on a quarterly basis and identify what bad habits to eliminate and what new habits to adopt. *Atomic Habits* by James Clear offers a fantastic framework for breaking bad habits and creating great ones.

The premise of the book is that small actions (think about the smallest particle), consistently taken over time, produce massive (think atomic bomb) results. Based on extensive research, Clear offers a simple four step process to adopt a great habit: make it obvious, attractive, easy, and satisfying. Conversely, to break a bad habit: make it invisible, unattractive, difficult, and unsatisfying.

To make it obvious, create simple and clear instructions for yourself. I will exercise at 10:00 a.m. in my office. Ways of making a habit attractive include creating anticipation of a reward, and habit stacking—for instance, *after I do ten burpees, I will check Facebook; after I journal, I will go shopping.* You can also reframe it with benefits. For example, *I get to exercise*, not *I have to exercise.*

To make it easy, design the environment and use cues such as placing workout clothes and sneakers next to your bed at night. If you desire to draw, set out pencils at night. If you want to improve your diet, chop fruits and vegetables in advance. The goal is to reduce friction in the execution of the activity. Use your phone to create reminders. To make it satisfying, reward yourself, keep track, and celebrate. Most high performers never celebrate successes, but instead move on to the next challenge and the next. Acknowledging and celebrating even the smallest success with a literal pat on your back creates positive momentum.

Be honest with yourself about what drives you, what motivates you, and what your weaknesses are. Know what stories you're telling yourself and be willing to change the disempowering stories. Use these techniques to create great habits and get rid of bad ones.

If you miss a commitment, don't entertain the disempowering stories. Get back on track. If you are anything like me, you may be inclined to approach projects with passion in the beginning. The challenge is to keep going when it gets difficult or boring, including when you don't feel motivated, simply don't feel like it, or when your brain creates excuses not to do it. One way to counteract this is to embrace consistency and keep showing up: "Consistently good is better than occasionally great."

The Importance of No

To live a purposeful life, you must say no to things that don't align with your immigrace. I know, that sounds selfish, but in our increasingly busy world, with media and social media demanding our attention, it is essential that we manage our focus. Managing your focus prevents burnout, and burnout is real. Women are particularly prone to feeling overwhelmed. It's the generous instinct that causes us to give to everything and everyone till we have nothing else to give and the tank is empty. One of the best books on this is *Essentialism* by Greg McKeown. He offers a framework for analyzing the various opportunities that come our way and for staying focused, not only on actions that align with our purpose but on actions that are most essential for us to fulfill in the world. He also notes the importance of rest, play, and recovery, in order to avoid burnout.

The Complete Extraordinary Results Formula

There are foundational principles throughout this book. A simple rule I followed in sharing resources is not to simply share things I've read that resonated. I share resources that are confirmed by research, but that I have also read, learned, applied, iterated, and for which I've seen extraordinary results.

With that in mind, there's a very simple process that I've used to accomplish every major goal I've attained. The "what" may change, but the process is the same.

First, I define what I want and I write it down. Research has shown that writing down goals notably increases the rate of success. According to a study conducted by Dr. Gail Matthews, psychology professor at Dominican University, writing down goals (along with sharing them and being held accountable through a group or coach) increased the success rate by 33 percent. According to another study by David Kohl, professor emeritus at Virginia Tech: "80 percent of Americans report that they don't have goals. Some 16 percent say they do have goals, but they don't write them down. Less than 4 percent take the time to write down their goals, and less than 1 percent review them regularly. This small percentage of Americans, who write down goals and review them regularly, earn nine times more over the course of their lifetimes, than those who don't set goals."[1]

I set quarterly goals in every single area of life. More on this in "Your Wheel of Life" to follow. I'm specific and detailed in what I want to accomplish. I then revisit what I've written weekly and daily. Below are the seven steps:

1. Decide what I want and write it down.
2. Define why I want it.
3. Identify action steps (chunk it down).
4. Take massive action.
5. Expect the unexpected. Adjust my approach, as needed.

6. Celebrate.
7. Rinse and repeat.

Your Wheel of Life

One of the greatest challenges a lot of high-achieving people face is the sense of being out of balance. This is usually due to focusing exclusively on one area, to the detriment of others. For women, in particular, we may find ourselves throwing ourselves completely into one area and entirely ignoring areas we would actually love to see flourish.

You can avoid feeling out of balance by setting quarterly goals and checking in on them on a weekly basis. An excellent resource on this subject is *The 12 Week Year: Get More Done in 12 Weeks than Others Do in 12 Months* by Brian P. Moran and Michael Lennington.

In addition, Tony Robbins uses the metaphor of a wheel for the various parts of one's life because you need all the areas working together (not necessarily perfectly, but continually improving) in order to truly feel happy and fulfilled.

Quite often, setting goals and giving even a bit of focus to our most important intentions and aspirations goes a long way in addressing the sense of deficit or the sense of things being out of control. You can also think of your goals as a pyramid, with a hierarchy—number seven at the bottom and number one at the peak.

I set quarterly and weekly goals in the following categories:

1. Faith/Spirituality/Contribution (e.g., spiritual retreat; volunteer at church or food pantry)
2. Finances (e.g., set a financial target; identify an account to pay off)
3. Work/Career/Mission (e.g., professional goals/targets/deliverables)
4. Managing Time (e.g., how to focus your time, or time blocking to accomplish specific tasks)

5. Relationships (e.g., activities with family members; focus areas for kids)
6. Managing Emotions/Meaning (e.g., music; focus-of-the-day phrases)
7. Health/Wellness/Physical Body (e.g., working out; diet)

In this section, you'll meet a number of women who set massive goals and accomplished them. They didn't allow themselves to be limited in their dreams, and they didn't allow others' limitations to define for them what was possible:

- Albania Rosario, award-winning founder and creative director of Fashion Designers of Latin America, a platform that brings Latin American designers to the world stage. Albania shared how she embarked on her impossible dream of bringing Latin American designers to New Fashion week, and how she continues to blaze trials around the world.

- Maureen Umeh, senior media and political advisor, public relations expert, and Emmy Award–winning television journalist. Nigeria-born Maureen shares how she overcame her initial struggle with American pronunciations, how she forged ahead toward her goals in spite of naysayers, and how she continues to make a global impact through providing strategic political and media advice.

- Sanaz Hariri, orthopedic surgeon. Born in Iran and relocated to the United States shortly after the revolution, Sanaz shares important life lessons, drawn from that instability: detachment from material things and creating memories. Sanaz was never afraid to speak up and ask, and this helped shape her professional journey and success.

- Sandra Parrado, forensic partner, PriceWaterhouseCoopers. Philippines-born Sandee relocated to the United States when she was a teen and her father was in the army. She shares the importance of mindset shifts and playing to our strengths in order to lead.

7.
Blazing Trails on Runways All Over the World

| **ALBANIA ROSARIO,**
Founder, CEO, and Creative Director
of Fashion Designers of Latin America

Albania Rosario is a trailblazing visionary and global leader in fashion. She is the founder and creative director of Fashion Designers of Latin America (FDLA).

Albania is the woman who brought Latin designers to the world stage and the forefront of New York Fashion Week (NYFW) and around the world. She has been recognized in South Korea, eastern Europe, and Asia as hosting one of the best fashion platforms for Latinos in the world.

In addition to a range of talent from Latin America, FDLA has attracted a plethora of talent from around the globe, including designers such as Michael Costello, Marc Bouwer, Agatha Ruiz de la Prada, and most recently, Carolina Herrera.

Albania's background in advertising, marketing, and communications has helped her forge relationships with her local communities, bringing sponsors to her organization, including Delta Air Lines, Hispanic Federation, and Moët Hennessy USA.

She is also the president of FDLA Foundation Inc. and creator of the FDLA online academy, a nonprofit organization that provides a platform for students to enroll in fashion-related courses, events, and training at little to no cost.

Albania has partnered with Hogar Sanisi, an orphanage with children affected by AIDS in the Dominican Republic. She hosts and produces the most magical fashion shows for these children, providing them everything they need to be stars of the runway.

A FRIEND INVITED me to two of Albania's FDLA events, beginning in 2018. I was deeply inspired by what Albania had created, imprinting NYFW with the exquisite Latino stamp for posterity. In the midst of show production, media interviews, and flashing cameras at Google NYC, Albania and I didn't actually meet or speak at the shows.

We subsequently connected on social media and communicated for months before we met in person in 2019. I'd attended Prospanica New York's Top Latino Leaders Under 40 award at S&P Global on Water Street in NYC, at which Albania was one of the esteemed honorees. Our sisterhood was instantly formed.

Runway Dreams

The runway was familiar and conquered territory for Albania at a young age. She was a vivacious and tenacious little princess who was ready to take on the world. On the runways of Santo Domingo, Dominican Republic, Albania dominated fashion shows and pageants, often taking first place. Encouraged by her parents, two siblings, and throngs of supportive extended family and friends, in young Albania's heart, a big dream was born—to be a supermodel and walk the runways of NYC.

Albania's parents were her biggest mentors. They always taught her that you can be anyone. Her mama also taught her never to leave a competition without accomplishing something tangible or something she could be proud of. While her mama's persistence, which involved making a scene once when Albania was about to leave a competition without a prize, sometimes bordered on making Albania feel embarrassed, it instilled in her a core value that would serve her well later in life.

A Dream Redefined

Albania arrived to the United States when she was eighteen years old, and she didn't speak a single word of English. She attended Hunter College of the City University of New York.

With her passion for fashion, she also quickly signed up with a number of modeling agencies to help achieve that goal.

It was several years later, after paying thousands of dollars to manipulative agencies and individuals, that she realized it was highly unlikely that she would be a runway model in the United States. She wasn't tall enough and was considered too chunky. To her disappointment, the agencies knew this, but they still collected payments from her and strung her along.

Letting go of a lifelong dream can be devastating and depressing. Rather than becoming depressed, however, Albania realized she still loved fashion and didn't want to leave the industry without making an impact. So she started to ask herself some great questions: *How can I have an impact on this industry? How can I make sure I don't leave the fashion industry without putting my mark on it?*

Imprinting the Fashion Industry

Albania was working as a volunteer for NYFW shows when she noticed the lack of opportunities for emerging Latinos in the industry. She realized that she wanted to create a platform for Latin American fashion designers: "It was clear to me that I needed to do something, something to create more opportunities to allow emerging fashion designers to be part of the fashion circuit in New York City during NYFW." She created a powerful platform that connects and builds bridges of fashion and opportunities across Latin America. "I brought a fresh perspective to the fashion capital of the world," she says. "FDLA is that platform."

As part of Uptown Fashion Week, Albania partnered with some key local leaders and organizations, such as City Councilman of Washington Heights Ydanis Rodríguez, the Chamber of Commerce of Washington Heights & Inwood, New York-Presbyterian Hospital, and the City University of New York. She also partnered with Snapple and JPlaza Productions.

In Albania's words, the initial fashion shows as part of Uptown Fashion Week in Washington Heights were "disasters." She failed and failed again. It wasn't because she didn't have the right intentions; it was because she didn't have the budget. She had a massive dream that required a lot of resources to bring it to life. She was going broke, and people began to think she was going crazy as well.

And then she conceived the brilliant idea to partner with an airline, so they could fly the designers from Latin America to New York. Through her collaboration with Delta Air Lines, the designers now only need to bring their designs with them. Over the years, she's also partnered with other sponsors, such as Moët Hennessy USA and Hispanic Federation.

Her vision of celebrating Latin American designers encompasses various countries across the region and in the diaspora, including Venezuela, Haiti, Peru, Nicaragua, Honduras, Chile, and the Dominican Republic. Albania has gained global recognition, and beyond

NYC, she's taken this vision to other cities such as Miami, Florida and Dubai in the United Arab Emirates.

In her earlier years, being a volunteer gave Albania her first behind-the-scenes glimpse into the fashion industry. Today, she gives others the opportunity to get their own introductions to fashion by working with her as volunteers. She's now had the chance to work with so many wonderful people. Her volunteers see and understand the vision. Nothing great is ever achieved by a single person. Albania has an army who understand the what, why, and how.

Albania's Definition of Success

Success is having the skills and ability to help others make their dreams come true. When Albania is able to travel to Nicaragua and other parts of Latin America, bring those designers to the global stage, and help them make their dreams come true, that to her is success.

ALBANIA'S IMMIGRACE

- Trailblazing visionary and global leader on fashion
- Community leader and philanthropist

ALBANIA'S IMMIGEMS

◇ *Be resourceful.* Know what you know, but also know who knows what you don't know. When facing a challenge or obstacle, many stop at "I don't know." Albania is in the habit of asking herself, *I may not know this, but who do I know who may know this, or who knows someone who knows?* It's the power of resourcefulness and leveraging relationships.

◇ *Understand that nothing worth fighting for comes easy.* Always start with the end in mind. If you have a vision and you can conceive it, follow your vision. Once you follow your vision, you will have to make some sacrifices, but you don't have to settle for less.

◇ *Expect to fail again and again.* You will fall down, but the real question is, how quickly will you get up?

8.
A Powerful
Voice for Progress

MAUREEN UMEH
Senior Media and Political Advisor, Public Relations
Expert, and Emmy Award–Winning Television Journalist

Maureen Umeh has won multiple Emmy Awards as a television journalist with more than twenty-five years of experience reporting on national, international, business, and political news. She is a proven media and political specialist who has crafted wide-ranging political campaign strategies and provided media training for members of the US Congress. She has established and maintains a wide range of political and international contacts, and she advises nonprofit organizations with stakes in the African and Latinx communities on rebranding strategies. Maureen is a highly skilled negotiator with a proven ability to build cross-cultural relationships and to analyze and resolve complex issues. She is an expert in crisis management, social media planning and outreach, marketing and communications, image consulting, and speech writing and training. She is fluent in English and Igbo and is competent in conversational French.

Maureen is an anchor, reporter, host and executive producer for *Fox 5 Morning* in Washington, DC. She has anchored news programs and reported on the front lines of some of the biggest and world-changing stories of this century. Highlights include coverage of the 9/11 terrorist attack; daily live reports from the US White House, Capitol, and Pentagon; one-on-one interviews with various members of the US Congress; coverage of the Republican and Democratic National Conventions; political talk shows; investigations and reports on stories that have resulted in local laws being changed and that have won awards; and cohosting the number one rated morning news entertainment show in Washington, DC.

Maureen leads a full-scale media consulting firm that specializes in messaging and branding, particularly in the political realm. Examples include the successful launch of a media outreach campaign targeting African voters, the development of media strategies and training for several former and current US congressional members, and the crafting and leading of the presidential campaign of a Democratic Republic of the Congo (DRC) candidate. Maureen was recruited by a top political consulting firm to run for a congressional seat in 2008.

Her first full-time reporting job was at WCIA-TV in Champaign, Illinois. She also served as one of the main anchors for the late evening newscasts at WSPA-TV in Greenville and Spartanburg, South Carolina.

Maureen has served as chairwoman for the Upstate Leadership Council of the American Cancer Society, as the board president of the African Women's Cancer Awareness Association, and as president of the Upstate SC Chapter of the American Red Cross. She has also worked with nonprofit organizations including Big Brothers Big Sisters and Matthew House, an agency for disadvantaged youth. She is a professional member of the Screen Actors Guild–American Federation of Television and Radio Artists (SAG-AFTRA) and the National Association of Black Journalists (NABJ). She serves as a board member of the International Sheroes Forum and the West African Health Initiative.

Maureen is the recipient of several awards, including Emmy Awards for Best Investigative Series and Best Newscast, as well as awards from the South Carolina Broadcasters Association, the Illinois Broadcasters Association, and the National Association for the Advancement of Colored People (NAACP).

She is a journalism graduate of University of Illinois at Urbana-Champaign.

Of all her accomplishments, Maureen believes that being a mom to her daughter is the greatest. She describes it as the most frightening and exhilarating experience of her life, one that has also given her a depth and gravitas that she never expected.

MY BROTHER OBI introduced me to Maureen, and we spoke by phone. Maureen is warm and vibrant. She's deeply conscious of the responsibilities that come with her platform, and she uses her passion to give voice to the voiceless and make lasting change in the world.

Say What You Want to Say

"You said a bad word!" the six-year-old boy screamed. Maureen was confused! What had caused her classmate to hurl what, by all accounts, seemed like an unwarranted accusation? All little Maureen did was ask for a fork! Okay, maybe in Nigeria the r in fork isn't enunciated as clearly as it is in the United States. He'd heard a different four-letter word. She wished someone had clued her in on the finer details of American articulation before this embarrassing episode that remains engraved in her memory.

The Dream

Being a broadcast journalist was Maureen's lifelong dream. As one who knew early on that she wanted to be a broadcast journalist, she needed to be able to express herself without conveying unintended meanings.

Along with her family, Maureen came to the United States from Nigeria when she was six years old. Young Maureen quickly became aware that she spoke differently. It wasn't until later in life that she came to learn that Americans, too, depending on where they are born and raised, have different accents and idiosyncrasies in speech.

Watching the news as child in Chicago, she revered Bill Kurtis and Walter Jacobson. They were superheroes to her. Their superpowers? Giving voice to the voiceless. And that's what she wanted to do when she grew up.

Honing the Gift

Maureen began to practice speaking in front of a mirror. She mastered saying the word *fork* without eliciting unintended reactions. In high school and college, she read aloud to anyone who would let her. She volunteered for every reading opportunity, including newspapers and church bulletins. She simply would not stop reading!

In college, she identified and worked hard at opportunities that would prepare her for a role in journalism. She wrote for the university newspaper, worked at the television station, had a radio talk show, and even deejayed.

Upon graduation from college, Maureen got a full-time job at WCIA-TV in Champaign, Illinois. Her next role was serving as one of the main anchors for the late evening newscast at WSPA-TV in Greenville and Spartanburg, South Carolina.

The Leap

Maureen's childhood dream to become a journalist included a distinct desire to do so in the nation's capital. One of the defining moments for her was moving to the Washington, DC, area from South Carolina.

Maureen risked it all, leaving her position as the main anchor in South Carolina and moved to DC without first securing a job.

Why Journalism?

As a broadcast journalist, Maureen loves that her work affords her the opportunity to effect little and big change. She is also keenly aware of the accompanying responsibilities and her profession's ability to inflict harm. She is aware of the danger of personal bias in media reporting and the resulting societal distrust of the media. As people approach her with their everyday challenges, she learns something new. Maureen and her colleagues do not simply cover stories to bring light to them (whether they include changing behavior and regulatory policy or they are just helping tell a story), but they also seek to do their part to prevent what can be prevented.

Every Super-shero Has a Villain

Maureen's journey to being an Emmy Award–winning journalist was not full of cheerleaders. As a college student at the University of Illinois in Champaign, a professor told her that she was saddled with alterable and unalterable "problems" that would get in the way of her dream. First, she was a dark-skinned Black woman. This would make it nearly impossible for her to succeed in broadcast journalism, he said.

The alterable "problem"? Her last name, Umeh. The professor asked her, "Who would succeed on TV with a last name like that?" Maureen laughed as she repeated the question. The professor's advice: find a new dream. To Maureen, it was incomprehensible. The professor sounded no different from Charlie Brown's teacher: "Wah wah wah."

Maureen knew the professor's statements were a product of his own ignorance and limiting beliefs. Her commitment to her goals was unshaken. More notably, she was determined to achieve them while maintaining her uniqueness and grace.

A Powerful Voice for Progress

As a result of the powerful voice Maureen developed in media and television and through various philanthropic efforts, a defining moment was when a top Maryland consulting firm approached Maureen to run for political office in 2008. Although she ultimately decided not to run, this reinforced her commitment to use her voice to drive political change around the world.

Maureen has consulted on some of the most prominent campaigns in history, including media outreach on the 2008 presidential campaign of Barack Obama. She's also provided campaign and media strategy for gubernatorial and congressional elections. She's developed media strategies and training for several former and current US congressional members, and she has crafted and led the presidential campaign of a candidate in the Democratic Republic of the Congo (DRC). Maureen also leads change around the world through her work with an organization that identifies women leaders to run for political office across Africa and Latin America.

Maureen's Definition of Success

Success to Maureen "Isn't about a profession, wealth, or status. It's quite simply waking up every day content and grateful. When you have happiness, you truly have everything."

MAUREEN'S IMMIGRACE

- Senior media and political advisor
- Public relations expert
- Emmy Award–winning television journalist

MAUREEN'S IMMIGEMS

◇ *Be determined.* Ignore the naysayers. Have tunnel vision, and recklessly pursue your dreams.

◇ *Believe that you are destined for greatness.* Everyone has a purpose. Understand and believe in your own unique purpose.

◇ *Have a faith foundation.* Keep God first, and trust that you will fulfill your purpose.

9.
Wanting It More than Anyone Else

SANAZ HARIRI, MD
Orthopedic Surgeon

S anaz Hariri, MD, is an orthopedic surgeon. Dr. Hariri was two years old when her family fled Iran for the California Bay Area via Miami and Los Angeles ("Tehran-geles"). She graduated from Harvard Phi Beta Kappa and magna cum laude with a BA in history in 1999 and from Stanford with an MD in 2003, and she completed an orthopedic surgery residency at Harvard, a hip/knee replacement fellowship at Harvard's Massachusetts General Hospital (MGH) in 2009, and then a sports/arthroscopy fellowship at Stanford in 2010.

As an undergraduate at Harvard, Sanaz was selected to dance in the Harvard-Radcliffe Ballet Company; was ticket cochair of An Evening with Champions, which raised close to $100,000 for the Dana-Farber Cancer Institute; codirected the Harvard Emerging Literacy program, which organized students to tutor at Head Start programs; and interned with Senator Dianne Feinstein, focusing on healthcare economics, and then with Massachusetts Governor Paul Cellucci, focusing on regulatory economics. In medical school at

Stanford, Sanaz founded the Real World Medicine course, served as student coordinator of the Arbor Free Clinic, and was elected student representative to the Committee on Courses and Curriculum.

She is the recipient of numerous honors and awards, including the prestigious Paul & Daisy Soros Fellowship for New Americans, the American Association of Hip and Knee Surgeons (AAHKS) Health Policy Fellowship, the Detur Book Prize for "being a top achiever in Harvard academic Rank I," and the John Harvard Scholarship for "academic achievement of the highest distinction." She is a member of several professional organizations, including the American Academy of Orthopedic Surgeons (AAOS), the American Association of Hip and Knee Surgeons (AAHKS), and the American Orthopedic Society for Sports Medicine (AOSSM).

Dr. Hariri is an expert in minimally invasive techniques for shoulder and knee arthroscopy and knee replacement. She has treated players in many elite athletic organizations, including the Stanford football and basketball teams, the United Football League, and the San Jose Ballet.

Her practice includes treating the elite athlete striving to return to the highest level of competition, the recreational athlete looking to return to an active lifestyle, and the elderly patient wanting to enjoy the activities of daily life without pain.

SANAZ AND MY brother, Obi, attended the Stanford University School of Medicine around the same time, both ultimately specializing in orthopedic surgery. An incredible combination of brains and beauty, Sanaz readily agreed to be interviewed for this project. Her passion for excellence is deeply inspiring.

Lessons from a Notebook

Protests. Strikes. Chaos in the streets. The burning of Rex Cinema. These events eventually led to the Iranian Revolution. By January 1979, Shah Mohammad Reza Pahlavi (the "Shah") fled Iran, never to return.

Sanaz's family lost virtually all of their personal property during the revolution, but powerful life lessons emerged that would shape Sanaz's worldview. The loss of one particular possession led to an unlikely gift. It was a notebook Sanaz's grandfather used to meticulously track every penny her mother, Azadeh, borrowed to fund her adventures. The notebook—and therefore symbolically the "debt"—disappeared, as had virtually all of their assets when revolutionaries raided their home.

Azadeh had a spectacular wedding gown that was handmade by a famous designer in Paris. The family's housekeeper had asked one of the family's relatives if she could borrow Azadeh's wedding gown for her daughter—just for the ceremony and the pictures, certainly not for the reception. The request seemed too absurd to pass on, but since Azadeh had heard about it through the family grapevine, she lent her dress to the housekeeper's daughter under one condition: that she had to wear it all night. Soon after the wedding, the revolution broke out. The wedding dress, safe at the housekeeper's home, survived. All the valuable contents of their own home were taken by looters. Something else the revolutionaries could not take: Azadeh's MBA from Indiana University, which fueled her post-revolution economic recovery.

Imbued with stories such as these at a young age, Sanaz's worldview formed: she learned that you could save up all the money in the world and hoard every material thing, and it could all be gone in an instant. The message was clear: invest in experiences and education, and do not grow attached to material possessions—assets are fleeting; memories and knowledge are forever.

The Gift of Uniqueness

Sanaz recalls the stress of coming to the United States during the Iranian Revolution. She was only two years old. Her family made the decision to "temporarily" relocate to the United States until the political conditions in Iran stabilized. There was hope—in fact certainty—that President Jimmy Carter would reinstate the Shah. That never happened.

Azadeh had already earned an MBA from Indiana University, and Sanaz's father, Farzam, had doggedly earned a BA from UCLA, having earned a full scholarship with his outstanding scores on an Iranian national exam in high school and while working full-time during college. Sanaz is grateful that the family's educational foundation gave her a head start in the immigrant experience, as both parents had proficiency in English and the American culture.

As an immigrant, by definition, you are different. Sanaz grew up in a homogenous neighborhood before the immigrant influx of the Silicon Valley boom, and she attended Catholic school, where she received a phenomenal education, but was the only person in her class who went to the library during confirmation classes—a boon for this avid reader.

Sanaz advises young immigrants to cherish what makes them different: "As an adult, being different is cool, exotic, and beautiful. However, most children just want to fit in, and differences are therefore often painful and something to be concealed. My advice to young immigrant children is to realize how lucky they are to be unique. Standing out for being you is thrilling and amazing—or at least, realize it will eventually feel amazing!"

Her advice to parents is to consider the impact that a child's surroundings and experiences could have on them. A psychiatry professor in medical school postulated that childhood is like walking through a field of exploding mines. Adulthood is the process of walking right back through that old minefield, either falling into those craters or figuring out ways to walk around them. Parents should try to minimize those craters and augment the coping mechanisms needed to skirt them. The key is to be mindful of the child's world and thought processes.

Trading Football for Surgery

Sanaz's family had season tickets to the San Francisco 49ers, and at eight years old, she just knew that her calling was to be a kicker in the National Football League (NFL). Let me put this into context: Sanaz as an adult is five foot four and weighs 115 pounds. But despite her small size, she practiced kicking for hours every day. One day, her brother Baha, who is three years her junior, on a whim, kicked the ball many times farther than she had ever done in her months of practice. She walked off the field dejected. That dream was dead.

Not long after, she was watching the NFL postgame show and saw the team doctor, Dr. Michael Dillingham, wearing a Super Bowl ring. She noticed him on the sidelines of games. A new dream was born.

From that moment as an eight-year old, everything in her life was measured against whether or not it would support her goal to be an orthopedic surgeon. She needed to get the best grade on every quiz and test because she could not let an exam get in the way of her dream. Even if she had a solid A in a class, she did not let a single extra-credit opportunity escape. Her eighth-grade thesis was a comparison of injury rates and patterns for NFL athletes on natural grass versus artificial turf. Eighth grade!

Don't Be Afraid to Ask

To research her eighth-grade thesis, Sanaz reached out to the San Jose Sharks team doctor, Dr. Arthur Ting, for an interview. It seemed natural to Sanaz to reach out to him. She was undaunted by his stature. He happily agreed, giving her rare insights from his unique experiences.

Similarly, one night, young Sanaz stayed late after her ballet class to catch another mentor, Dr. Amy Ladd, after her adult evening ballet class. She was ten years old, and she wanted Dr. Ladd's advice on how to be like her—how to become an orthopedic surgeon. Over a decade later, Sanaz sought out Dr. Ladd at Stanford, where she was starting medical school. She wondered if she remembered her—of course she did! Who can forget a ten-year-old so sincerely curious and determined? Sanaz teamed up with Dr. Ladd for a research program as a medical student, and Dr. Ladd championed Sanaz's application to Harvard for residency, as Dr. Ladd herself had been a noteworthy fellow there.

In high school, Sanaz reached out to Dr. Dillingham (the NFL team doctor), who graciously let her shadow him. She studied his diagnostic maneuvers and easy rapport with patients, picked up on patterns of diagnosis and treatment, and was inspired by his unrelenting dedication to continuing education and research to provide the best possible patient care.

When she was accepted into Harvard, Dr. Dillingham gave her genius advice—consider a major in history, as he had done at Stanford, as it would help sharpen her communication and relational skills. That settled it: Sanaz became a history major, requiring disciplined planning from the start in order to fulfill her pre-med requirements as electives so as to graduate in four years.

Sanaz emphasizes the importance of seeking out mentors. Her family was populated with businessmen. If folks around you do not know enough to support your goals, seek out mentors who do.

A Champion's Mindset

Sanaz has been consistently guided by the mindset that you can have something if you want it more than anyone else and if you want it to the detriment of everything else. With this mindset, there is no way you will not eventually achieve your goals.

There are social implications. You sacrifice and miss out on things you want a whole lot less than your dreams—time and outings with friends and family, entertainment (e.g., television shows, movies, concerts), and often sleep. (Somehow, watching football was allowed because she considered it "research," and there was time during commercial breaks to study. Another "research" indulgence: her favorite class in high school was Sports Literature, of course. Dr. Lenore Horowitz, the teacher, expertly honed Sanaz's writing skills as nobody had done before. Those writing skills—unique particularly among doctors—made her a standout medical student, resident, and fellow.)

When Sanaz sets out to do something, she seeks to be the best at it. Her capacity to work until she is the best at what she does is epic. For example, she performs a rather narrow range of surgeries— only those procedures at which she knows she is as good as the best. For everything else, she refers the patient to the best qualified colleague.

Sanaz also believes we should only be in competition with ourselves. Life is not a zero-sum game. That zero-sum-game mentality is a petty and destructive worldview that does not contribute to the betterment of society and civilization and is simply false. Others' success does not detract from yours and should uplift and inspire you. Sanaz chose Stanford for medical school in large part because it had no grades, which allowed classmates to relax and collaborate. Work collaboratively and generously with those around you. Generosity inevitably circles back to you.

For example, a physical therapist trying to further his career by writing a textbook approached the Harvard orthopedic surgery chairman and asked him to contribute a chapter to his book—the chairman's name associated with the book would be invaluable. The chairman, busy with myriad responsibilities, advised the therapist to approach his best resident writer—Sanaz—to coauthor the chapter. Writing this chapter would not in any foreseeable way enhance Sanaz's career, but she admired the therapist's ambition and could not bear to crush his hopes. She had a rare weekend off, and she buried herself for two days and nights researching, writing, and rewriting that chapter. The therapist and chairman were stunned that the chapter had been written so quickly and so thoroughly.

That generosity was returned to Sanaz under the most surprising and unlikely of circumstances. Sanaz once had a goal to be a sports fellow at Standford. On the glorious day that her dream fellowship was offered to her, Dr. Marc Safran, the fellowship director, told Sanaz that many powerful people at the Harvard and Stanford orthopedic programs had written letters or called him on her behalf, but the deciding factor was the ringing endorsement of that Harvard therapist, whom Dr. Safran had reached out to for input, and who, as it turned out, was Dr. Safran's roommate as an undergraduate at UCLA.

Be Ready to Build—And Rebuild

For better or for worse, the immigrant mindset is often tinged with feeling of uncertainty and instability—particularly for those who survived a revolution. Sanaz reports that she has been fueled by a deep desire to establish stability and to gain knowledge and skills that would transcend circumstances. Her single-minded obsession with education—and choice of surgery as a career—can thus be understood. Part of Sanaz's joy in working is demonstrating work ethic and drive to her twin eight-year-old boys, Nate and Jackson. Her belief is that those pillars of success cannot be effectively preached—they must be lived.

In her own family history, she recalls the family lore of her maternal great-grandfather, Jalal Sadat Tehrani, starting off as a little boy selling socks on a blanket outside a bazaar in Tehran and working his way up to becoming a major textile and real estate magnate. Sanaz was acutely aware of her parents losing almost all of their assets during the Iranian Revolution in 1979, trying to rebuild in Miami, losing their small start-up money in an ill-fated real estate venture, and then again trying to rebuild in Los Angeles with an export/import company that went bankrupt—culminating in the foreclosure of their home. The next stop? Los Altos, California, living in the basement of her maternal grandparents' home, where Sanaz marveled at how wealthy they must have been because they owned an Encyclopedia Britannica collection that she could not put down. And, finally, they rebuilt again—this time a successful wholesale grocery business, Pacific Groservice, Inc. (PGI). Life is about building, rolling up one's sleeves to rebuild as many times as necessary, and, in preparation, gaining the education and skills needed to be ready for whatever may come.

Sanaz's Definition of Success

Sanaz defines success as identifying your goal and then working strategically with epic determination toward that goal. There is immense satisfaction in knowing that there was nothing else you could have done and that no one else could possibly have worked harder.

SANAZ'S IMMIGRACE

- Preeminent orthopedic surgeon

SANAZ'S IMMIGEMS

◈ *Remember that you can come from nothing and be anything here.* Here is Sanaz's powerful reminder to immigrant women: "The immigrant experience humbles you and also shows you that if you are willing, there is virtually nothing you cannot achieve. American society is not perfect. It is not color-blind or gender-neutral. It is a collection of imperfect humans. But the ideal of America is the best the world has to offer. And the realization of that ideal is closer with each generation. You can come from nothing and be anything. So think big, plan big, and back it up with massive, unwavering action. Create. Contribute. Be a part of our country's—and our civilization's—march forward."

◊ *Give respect.* Treat everyone with respect, no matter their rung in the ladder. The dignity of a job well done is beautiful and deserves respect in all walks of life. As a surgeon, Sanaz has painstakingly built a team that treats their patients as if they were their own mothers or fathers. Surrounding oneself with people of such character at each level—and demonstrating your respect for their contribution—is inspiring and fulfilling.

◊ *Be useful.* The best way to be promoted is to figure out how you can lighten the load of those above you. The question "How can I make your life easier?" is often unexpected and always powerful. The "boss" may not immediately know the answer because the question may be so unexpected—but eventually a path to being useful can emerge. For Sanaz, she found that helping her attending physicians with research projects and writing chapters translated into more active mentorship in clinic and in the operating room, which enhanced her education. And she reminds us to never wait for a promotion to do more. A promotion is often an acknowledgement of what you already do—particularly for women who, in her observations, are less often promoted for their promise than for their achievements.

10.
Ready or Not, Here You Go

SANDRA "SANDEE" PARRADO
Partner at PricewaterhouseCoopers (PwC)

S andee Parrado has over twenty years of experience in providing consulting services. She leads a variety of engagements, with a focus on forensic investigations of fraud and accounting matters, Foreign Corrupt Practices Act (FCPA) investigations and anti-corruption compliance, money laundering lookback investigations, as well as litigation support and troubled company services.

Sandee's experience in matters related to foreign corrupt practices, including investigations, premerger due diligence, and audit program development and execution, has involved multinational companies in financial services, aerospace and defense, engineering and construction, industrial products, consumer products, and technology industries.

Sandee's experience in forensic accounting has included investigations into highly complex frauds and accounting irregularities in the automotive industry, cable and telecommunications companies, construction, vacation ownership, consumer electronics, and hardware manufacturers.

Sandee is also experienced in litigation matters, including damage valuations in the areas of intellectual property and antitrust. She has also prepared damage analyses and expert reports relating to patent, copyright, and trademark infringement, misappropriation of trade secrets, breach of contract, labor disputes, and antitrust claims.

Sandee obtained a Bachelor of Science in economics from the Wharton School of the University of Pennsylvania. Her concentrations were in finance, accounting, and operations and information management. She is a certified public accountant.

I FIRST SAW Sandee at an FCPA conference in New York City where she was a panelist. Twenty-plus years into her consulting career and a forensics partner at PwC, Sandee was all of five feet and one inch, and her diminutive stature was swallowed by the speaker's dais as she took her seat, yet she commanded the room and spoke with such credibility and executive presence. More than two years later, I had the opportunity to work closely with her on a project. I was impressed by Sandee's broad expertise, her oversight of a highly competent, high-performing team, and their firm commitment to delivering a high-quality product. Sandee and I have also served as co-panelists at conferences and share best practices in the world-changing area of anti-corruption. When I learned that Sandee was born in the Philippines, I couldn't wait to hear her story.

What Do You Want?

"Do you want to be a partner?" One of Sandee's coaches asked her one pivotal day at lunch. "Of course I do!" Someone watching closely would have recognized in her too-strident response that Sandee's defenses were speaking. In truth, she never told herself she wanted to be partner. That was for other people. She kept her nose to the grindstone and did a great job. She may have been good at seven out of ten things, but she worried too much about the three that she didn't excel at, and she let those three determine what she thought was possible. We women tend to overemphasize our weaknesses. But in that moment, when Sandee was faced with the fork in the road, between a yes and a no to such an existential career question, there was only one answer: "Of course I do!" However, silently, what was even louder than the bluster were the doubts in her head, like knives slashing self-inflicted wounds to cut herself down to size: *Will I be good? What if I fail?* When we find ourselves in that quiet moment of taking that step into the next chapter, Sandee notes the importance of believing in ourselves even when our own minds test our confidence, of preparing to best equip ourselves in the journey, of playing to our strengths and not our weaknesses, and of being willing—maybe even willing ourselves—to take that leap of faith to advance our lives and careers to the next level.

Although Sandee leads with such grace and authority, she notes that making partner at PwC wasn't part of a grand master plan. When she'd originally applied to PwC upon graduation from college, she didn't get the job. These twists and turns in the journey of life and career that allowed Sandee to understand and pursue what she wanted (at times coming full circle), and her tenacity to keep going, mirror every immigrant woman's journey.

Sacrifice for Freedom and Opportunity

For Sandee, the answer to the question "Do you want to be a partner?" and all the fear and hope and leaps of faith that come with confronting that question had been shaped by the forces of history and sacrifice and the appreciation that hardships forge strength. For Sandee, her story is the story of a Filipino people and a family.

Sandee's family came to the United States in 1985 from the Philippines. Her grandfather was in the US Army and fought alongside the United States during WWII, which helped in some way when her mother applied for a US green card. The immigration process took what seemed like forever, as it so often does, but her mother eventually completed it. Sandee's father, meanwhile, was reluctant to move to the United States, but her parents ultimately embraced the trials of starting over because of the promise of an idea called the American Dream.

But choosing the American Dream meant leaving a life that was comfortable. In the Philippines, Sandee's parents were successful senior executives in their fields. At home, the family had three live-in maids, one for each child. The maids cooked, cleaned, and took care of the house. Sandee and her siblings "helped" the maids, not because the kids had chores or were doing actual work, but because it was all fun and games. It was fun to do laundry and help out around the house when you could stop anytime, not do a good job, and not finish the work because it was all a game of pretend and others were there to take care of everything.

That life of leisure and comfort soon started to change. In August 1983, Benigno "Ninoy" Simeon Aquino Jr., who served as a senator of the Philippines and governor of the province of Tarlac, was assassinated at Manila International Airport upon his return from his self-imposed exile. Ninoy was a staunch critic of the then current President (and de facto dictator) Ferdinand Marcos. Ninoy was in exile to preserve his life and freedom; he was returning to the Philippines knowing that he was giving up both. (Ninoy was also the husband of Corazon Aquino—who, after his death, became president of the Philippines—and father of a later President, Benigno Aquino III.)

The Philippines was deep into a two-decade dictatorship under the Marcos regime, but Ninoy Aquino's assassination awakened the Filipino spirit from its resigned endurance of a totalitarian rule. There was much uncertainty in the wake of Ninoy's killing. Inflation skyrocketed, which meant weekly grocery shopping in order to convert a depreciating currency into consumables. Sandee witnessed her family stuffing every pantry full of groceries, as if Armageddon was upon them, if only because the value of money was evaporating with every passing day. They were continually in what seemed like disaster-preparation mode.

That coveted green card—the golden ticket to the American Dream—came around this time of national upheaval. Her parents made the decision for Sandee's mom to leave first for the United States. At that time in 1983, her mom was leaving at the height of her career; she was leaving her kids and the comforts of a well-supported household; and she was leaving alone to chart the course for the family. Sandee's dad was left behind in the Philippines with the children to wind down a chapter that had been marked by success and security. Only years later did Sandee and her younger sister and brother appreciate that this was not just a winding down of a career built from scratch, but also the sacrificing and letting go of an existence and life connections. Her dad left behind his parents, whom he would never see alive again.

During this long kiss goodbye, communication with Sandee's mom was difficult and sporadic because there were no cell phones at the time. Her mom started out on the West Coast, then moved to Fair Lawn, New Jersey. She selected Fair Lawn because it had a great public school system that would ensure the children would get a good education, which would serve as the foundation for their future.

In those initial days, Sandee's mom did what she had to do to earn a living. She had gone from being a successful human resources executive at a multinational company, with lots of domestic help, to being a secretary to a Filipino businessman. At night, she worked at QuickChek, a franchise convenience store.

Reunited in Fair Lawn

Approximately a year and a half later, when Sandee was about thirteen years old, the rest of the family joined Sandee's mom in the United States. Sandee's dad went from being a senior executive in the Philippines, working for a multinational company whose major client was McDonald's, to working in the United States as a manager at McDonald's. The family lived in the basement of the home of another Filipino family. The kids had to do chores—real chores this time—and it wasn't much fun anymore.

Sandee's transition from the East to the West as a budding teenager was not an easy one. In the Philippines, Sandee attended an all-girls school run by nuns. Respect, obedience, and humility were paramount. But the way of the West was different. On her first day of school in Fair Lawn, New Jersey, she felt like a fish on dry land. She stood by herself at the bus stop and heard the other kids whispering about "the new kid." Class was different too. In the Philippines, kids stood up to address the class. It was much less formal in the United States, so a slight Asian girl reflexively standing up to answer a teacher's question was startling and strange to her American classmates. Thirteen-year-old Sandee also thought it was awkward to hear other girls speaking about boys at such a young age—this wasn't commonplace among her friends back home. Although Sandee doesn't recall being pushed to get good grades, she excelled at school. She also played sports: volleyball and track. It turns out that the language of sports was the same and transcended cultural differences. Sports served the double purpose of shielding her from being too nerdy and from getting picked on. They also taught her valuable life skills—trying, failing, and building resilience.

Blending Assets

Sandee views being an immigrant as an asset. To have lived the world from its two halves has given her the unique gift of dexterity. She blends the best of western and eastern cultures, though the blending can also be a grind on the psyche. Growing up, she was taught respect for elders and for authority, but succeeding in the United States often requires slightly different—and sometimes opposite—skill sets. Most notably, in her chosen field of forensics, questioning and challenging discussions, notwithstanding authority, is needed for success. Additionally, if humility and sacrifice were ingrained in her formative years, putting her capabilities on display and advocating for herself have been acquired and critical skill sets. Being aware that there are two edges of the sword and having the flexibility and awareness to wield either side is critical for immigrant women. Arguably, this dexterity in navigating the landscape is more than critical . . . it is an advantage, and immigrant women have this limitless well to tap into!

Sandee's Definition of Success

Sandee defines success as having peace and peace of mind. Having been through chaos and upheaval as an immigrant family, the absence of angst feels like success. At work, when things are under control, and even in the midst of conflict, when there is a recovery plan, that feels like success. At home and for her family, meeting the world on the terms that are of one's choosing also provides the peace of mind that defines success.

SANDEE'S IMMIGRACE

- Strategic global business advisor
- Creator of leaders

SANDEE'S IMMIGEMS

- ◈ *Don't focus on your limitations.* As women, we tend to focus on our limitations, but our true power comes from focusing on our strengths and harnessing them.

- ◈ *Create more leaders.* The true measure of a leader is developing others. Organizations do not need only one great person.

They need great people, teams of them. Give your team the opportunity to succeed or fail. Trust them with your reputation, knowing that their performance will reflect on you. As a leader, you must be comfortable with assessing risk, asking the right questions, thinking through options, and, yes, experiencing failure.

◇ *Have grit.* You only fail when you give up. Everything else is part of the journey to help make you better!

Immigrace Journal

Ready, Set, Goals!

1. What are my goals for this quarter?

    a. Faith/Spirituality/Contribution

    _____

    _____

    _____

    b. Finances

    _____

    _____

    _____

    c. Work/Career/Mission

    _____

    _____

    _____

    d. Managing Time

    _____

    _____

    _____

e. Relationships

_____

_____

_____

f. Managing Emotions/Meaning

_____

_____

_____

g. Health/Wellness/Physical Body

_____

_____

_____

2. Fighting for My Legacy

a. Define it. What do I want my life to stand for?

_____

_____

_____

b. How can I live my legacy? Not just leave a legacy when I'm gone, but how can I live a life of legacy?

_____

_____

_____

c. How do I wish to write my life story and what are my most important outcomes?

_____

_____

_____

d. How do I choose to focus—my time, my resources, and my talents?

_____

_____

_____

e. What must I eliminate?

_____

_____

_____

f. What can I do that will tap into my unique background and interests?

_____

_____

_____

g. Is it time for a radical change, and how can I begin to invest in a new direction?

_____

_____

_____

h. Who must I become in order to live a meaningful and impactful life?

_____

_____

_____

3. Habits Audit

    a. What are the top three great habits I would love to keep:

        _____

        _____

        _____

    b. What are the top three bad habits I would love to change:

        _____

        _____

        _____

PART IV
Transform Failure

Sanya Richards-Ross is convinced that failure, that bitter ingredient, is likely the most essential ingredient in the recipe for success. You must have heard that failure is a teacher. Nike Master Trainer Brian Nunez, Founder and Owner of Fitness Never Sleeps (FNS) Training Center notes that "the greatest lessons are learned through the pain." The question is how to find the bravery to discover the lessons that are hidden in the pain.

Failures show up in different forms and sizes. You might fail to hit the mark on those large, long-term goals, or there might also be smaller disappointments along the way. There might be rejections, noes, and instances when things don't go according to plan or contradict your expected outcomes. Failure could also include the loss of a job, an unsuccessful job interview, not getting that promotion, or not achieving the desired result on a big project.

There are innumerable examples of successful people who endured failure along the way. Indeed, these are guaranteed legs in the journey. They are not detours. They are the journey. In order to hit the game winning shots, legendary basketball players such as

Michael Jordan and Kobe Bryant missed thousands of shots. Author Jack Canfield (of the wildly popular Chicken Soup for the Soul series) encountered astonishing rejection before his equally astonishing successes.

As an initial matter, most people do not set about accomplishing great things due to a fear of failure. To fail at something can be disappointing, embarrassing, and disillusioning. And some may be of the opinion that, the greater the endeavor, the greater the embarrassment that results from failure. With a perspective like this, trying becomes daunting and it's more attractive to retreat from those big dreams.

We must remember that all important endeavors require some degree of risk taking. The risk includes the probability that things won't work out as planned. One of the ways to reduce the probability of things not working out is to do just that—plan. Planning should include mapping out possible scenarios, considering alternative options and mitigants, and assessing risk, based on research and available information. Define the price—what's the worst that could happen? Clarify the cost—what resources are required? What aspects of this decision rely on hope? Hope shouldn't replace prudence and proper diligence.

Clarity is power because it gives you a sense of where you are and what you may encounter in the the future. Unfortunately, planning doesn't transport you into the future and reveal all possible outcomes, but it increases your level of engagement, gives you greater certainty, and as a result, increases the probability of success.

Whether or not the best-case scenario comes to pass, there'll certainly be lessons. It is often better to regret something you've done, rather than to regret something you didn't do, and to wonder about what could or may have been.

When we do encounter failure along the way, part of what we want to cultivate is a mindset that doesn't allow the failures to deter us from our big goals.

It is also helpful to view challenges from different angles. When things go wrong, we have a tendency to view things from the worst perspective. Our fears create the worst-case scenario. For example, you're working on a project. You reach out to someone in your field whom you greatly admire to participate in it. They decline participation. The mental creation of the worst-case scenario would go something like this: *This entire project will be a failure. I will never find the right people to support the project. I always ruin the important things. I am such a failure!*

You can shift your perspective by viewing the situation differently: *This wasn't the right time for her. I will find the right people to collaborate with. I will find the right resources to support me. I am committed to this project because of how much it will contribute to my field and to others. I will figure this out!*

Find the optimistic angle, one little shift at a time. These little shifts help us discipline our disappointments, so to speak, ensuring that they do not derail us. If you have a difficult time viewing things from different or more optimistic perspectives, seek out the input of a trusted advisor, mentor, or friend.

This section is about transforming the experiences we may define as failures and how we can use them to continually support our journeys. As the sections in the book are mutually reinforcing, the foundational principles noted in Sections II and III are enormously useful in transforming failure.

In this section, you'll read the stories of three women and how they redefined certain experiences in their lives that could otherwise have been characterized as failures:

- Sanya Richards-Ross, four-time Olympic-gold-medal-winning track-and-field athlete and TV personality. Jamaica-born Sanya shares how her failures shaped her great successes. Drawing from her experiences with career-disrupting illness and a disappointing performance at the 2008 Olympics, she shares insights about how failure is the essential ingredient for success and how to tap into our limitless potential in the moments when we are tempted to "quit digging" because we do not realize that the pot of gold is right around the corner.

- Dee Poku, social entrepreneur and women's advocate. Ghana-born and UK-raised Dee shares the importance of tapping into one's network, and how a mentor taught her the invaluable lesson to never take no for an answer.

- Nkechi Akunwafor, certified public accountant (CPA) and a director of corporate accounting. Nigeria-born Nkechi shares her story of being a teenager who relocated to the United States without family and was transported from one aunt to the next. She tells how she turned things around, from being on academic probation in her sophomore year in college to receiving job offers from all "Big Four" accounting firms. She also shares lessons from her rapid professional growth in corporate America.

11.
Failure
Is Golden

SANYA RICHARDS-ROSS
Four-Time Olympic-Gold-Medal-Winning
Track-and-Field Athlete and TV Personality

S anya Richards-Ross is one of the world's fastest female track-and-field athletes. She brought home her first individual Olympic gold medal in 2012 for the 400 meters. Sanya had previously won gold as part of the 4x400-meters relay team three consecutive times.

Sanya is the founder of MommiNation, an online community that provides reliable resources to support mothers. She is also the cohost of *Central Ave TV*, a weekly, nationally syndicated television series.

Sanya was named Visa Humanitarian of the Year in 2005, and her namesake charity, the Sanya Richards-Ross Fast Track Program, benefits children in need in her native country, Jamaica. Created in 2007, the program combines literacy and numeracy and promotes an active and healthy lifestyle through sports. Sanya's wedding to her college sweetheart, Aaron Ross, a two-time Super Bowl champion cornerback with the New York Giants, was featured on the television show *Platinum Weddings*. Sanya's docuseries, *Glam & Gold*, aired on We TV in 2013 and chronicled her life as she juggled appearances, a business, and family life. She's also the author of *Chasing Grace: What the Quarter Mile Has Taught Me about God and Life.*

SANYA MADE TIME to speak to me by phone one afternoon from her home in Texas, after returning from a run. Her warmth and passion were readily apparent, and she laughed easily. I also sensed that she's deeply grounded, yet driven—she knows who she is and knows what she wants out of life.

ONE SWELTERING AFTERNOON at St. Thomas Aquinas High School in South Florida, a fight ensued outside the cafeteria. A large group of students gathered around, anxious and excited to learn what had happened.

Sanya was one of two students who had seen the entire incident. She launched into replay mode—who said what, to whom, and how each reacted. She eventually arrived at the climax of the narrative: who struck the first punch.

"Then he tumped him!" Sanya shared.

Silence. Her fellow students were at a loss. *Tumped?*

"He did what?" they asked.

Sanya meant to say *punched*, but *tump* is the Jamaican Patois slang word for *punched*. Sanya suddenly longed to disappear into the ground. She realized that in the midst of all the excitement, her accent was more pronounced, and she hadn't taken the time to think through her choice of words. She viewed her accent as a distraction during conversations. She'd rather stand out for other reasons, she thought.

However, her schoolmates seemed to love her distinct Jamaican accent, and they'd often urge her to speak more or repeat a statement because they loved the sound of her lilting voice. While she was unafraid to speak up, Sanya didn't want to be seen as different.

Sanya resolved to get rid of her accent. She watched movies, television shows, and commercials. She also practiced with much dedication. This, along with playing sports like basketball and running track, helped her find her ground.

Living Her Passion

Sanya grew up in Kingston, Jamaica. Track and field and soccer are the two biggest sports in Jamaica, so Sanya began to run track at age seven. Two years later, Sanya's dreams were set. At age nine, her grade school teacher asked the students to write what they wanted to be when they grew up. Sanya wrote, "an Olympic champion."

Sanya's aunt, who lived in Florida for years, urged Sanya's parents to relocate to the United States. When Sanya was twelve, they did so, along with Sanya and her younger sister, Shari.

The move was a major adjustment for the family. Like most pre-teens, Sanya was anxious to fit in. She was stressed out because she had worn uniforms in Jamaica, but her middle school in Florida didn't require them. So she felt unrelenting pressure about what to wear to school every day.

Sports gave her a path into people's hearts. They also put her at the forefront of the school's attention. "Everyone loves a great athlete," Sanya told me with a chuckle.

Before long, she had great success in high school athletics, breaking national records and leading her school to four consecutive state track-and-field championships, all while maintaining a 4.0 GPA. She was the number one track recruit out of high school. As a sophomore at the University of Texas at Austin, she made the Olympic track-and-field team, and she won her first Olympic gold medal as part of the US 4x400-meter relay team in 2004.

Facing Adversity

In 2007, Sanya faced one of the greatest physical challenges of her life: mouth ulcers, skin lesions, intense joint pain, and extreme fatigue. Her body was attacking itself. Even worse, her symptoms stumped doctors. Seven doctors later, she was diagnosed with a rare autoimmune disease called Behcet's syndrome.

Her family didn't allow her to become depressed and helped her hold on to her vision for individual Olympic gold. At times, the disease seemed insurmountable. At one time, the ulcers were so severe that she couldn't speak and would write notes to her father. Sometimes she'd run with a cup in her mouth, to prevent her teeth from grinding. It would take a whole lot more than lesions and ulcers to keep her from her dreams.

Sanya had a great year and was ranked number one in the national and qualifying 400-meter races for the Olympics. She headed into the 2008 Beijing Olympics as the favored athlete for individual gold. She had dreamed of this since she was nine. During the 400-meter race, she was distracted and suddenly felt a cramp in her leg. In an instant, others ran past her. She won bronze, but she felt like an epic failure.

She chose not to let her desire to be the best become a burden. She resolved to return to the basics, to remind herself why she loved running, and to enjoy running for the pure joy of pushing herself to her ultimate best. The next season she won her first World Championship title at 400m, and now, all she had to do was continue this for another three years and win Olympic gold in 2012.

Things didn't quite work out as planned. In 2010, as Sanya prepared for the 2012 Olympics, she pulled a muscle. Sanya was forced to end the season early and take some time off. The silver lining in that year was her marriage to professional football player Aaron Ross, her college sweetheart.

The year 2011 proved to be the worst of Sanya's professional career. She had recovered physically, but she wasn't prepared for the mental residue that being injured and sidelined for a year brought with it. Although she worked hard that year, she still came up short, finishing seventh at the World Outdoor Championships.

Achieving Her Lifelong Dream

The next season, Sanya did a number of things differently. She trained with male track-and-field athletes and regularly met with a sports psychologist to mentally prepare herself. She focused on the one weakness in her game and resolved to make it her strength. She drowned out the naysayers and focused on her ultimate goal.

When Sanya arrived at the London Olympics in 2012, she was mentally and physically prepared. Unlike in 2008, she didn't listen to the screaming crowds, the critics, or those keeping score. She didn't look up at the intimidating Olympic rings. And she finally won gold in the individual 400-meter event.

Sanya is convinced that failure, the bitter component, is likely the most essential ingredient in the recipe for success. She wouldn't be the athlete she is today if she hadn't experienced the failures that preceded the success.

She also firmly believes that in creating and fulfilling our dreams, we give others permission to do the same. At her commencement speech to the University of Texas graduating class of 2013, she offered the following advice:

> There are millions of people on this earth, but there is only one you. What the world needs is your vision, your creativity, your character, your fearlessness, your passion. No, you won't always feel ready for every opportunity, and no, you won't always win. But life is always preparing us for what God has next. . . . I challenge you too to write your own speech. Don't allow fear or doubt to make you miss out on your greatest opportunities. As I've made this promise to myself to embrace failures and life's obstacles, as I open myself up to endless

possibilities, growth, and successes, I challenge every single one of you to make the same promise. Chart your own path, live your own dreams, write your own speech.

Staying Grounded

Sanya's family is her compass. They have accompanied and supported her through the high and low points. Her parents are her managers, her cousin is her public relations officer and stylist, and her sister is her hair stylist. Sanya is grateful that her family tells her the truth, no matter what. They especially don't hesitate to tell her when she's wrong. Sanya notes that quite often, celebrities and other high-profile people are surrounded by those who are afraid to be frank with them. But she counts her family—her loving compass—as one of her many blessings.

Sanya loves that her work allows her to travel and to see various parts of the world and experience different cultures. She remains closely connected to Jamaica. She visits often—for her charity efforts, for vacation, and to attend family events such as weddings.

One of the many aspects Sanya cherished about running was being out on the track. She loved feeling the rawness and toughness of the track beneath her feet. She loved to be challenged, to compete, and to excel. It gave her the opportunity to dig deep and strive for something significant. When she stepped on the track, she felt like she could do anything.

Although Sanya's path as a professional athlete was clear from an early age, her father always challenged her not to be one-dimensional. For instance, he encouraged her to be passionate about her studies, so she was. Her father's challenge also explains why today Sanya has numerous passions and excels in doing charity work, running a business, and serving as a spokesperson for various international brands such as Nike, BP, BMW, Citibank, and Nutrilite.

The Consummate Innovator

What does a fulfilled life look like after winning Olympic gold, not once, not twice or three times, but four times? Sanya is a devoted wife and mother, and she is also a consummate innovator. She deeply believes that success in one area of life spills over and feeds a desire to excel in other aspects of life. She continues to find ways to contribute, to live out successes in every area of her life, and to challenge herself to grow. She's the founder of MommiNation, an online community providing reliable and engaging content to support mothers in living out their dreams in work and family life. MommiNation provides fun and inspirational resources, as well as events to support moms' overall well-being. One example of MommiNation's various resources is the fitness challenge, which includes live workouts with a trainer, accompanied by reggae and soca music, and which moms can join from the comfort of their homes anywhere in the world.

Sanya is also the cohost of *Central Ave TV*, a weekly, nationally syndicated television series. In 2021, Sanya joined NBC's lineup as a sports analyst on the primetime coverage of the Tokyo Olympics.

Even with her many successes, Sanya continues to challenge herself and trusts that much more is yet to come.

Sanya's Definition of Success

According to Sanya, "Success is not about money or gold medals. At the very core, every individual knows who they are. You know you are great and you know your potential. Success is living out your potential in every area of your life, whether in family life, as an entrepreneur, or on the track."

SANYA'S IMMIGRACE

- Four-time Olympic-gold-medal winner
- Entrepreneur
- Innovator
- Philanthropist

SANYA'S IMMIGEMS

◇ *Don't be afraid.* Be bold and fearless in setting your goals. Don't allow the fear of being different hold you back from eing your boldest and best self. This is particularly true when you know you have something to give, whether it's a thought, an invention, or a solution to a problem. With the benefit of time and experience, and after reflecting on the "tumped" episode in high school, Sanya has realized that people are intrigued by difference, and that is an asset, if we're bold enough to leverage it.

◇ *Be adaptable.* Sanya's injuries and illnesses seemed to threaten the very core of her life's work—her physical apparatus. In adapting to those circumstances, she discovered a gem. She developed her mental muscle and experienced her true potential. The battles ultimately taught her to rely less on physical strength, and, in doing so, she became an even more outstanding athlete.

◇ *Be determined to achieve your goal.* Never give up. As Sanya said, "Success is a string of failing forward. We fail, but we keep going forward, and finally we land on success."

12.
Rejection Is Your Call to Action

| **DEE POKU-SPALDING**
Social Entrepreneur and Women's Advocate

Dee Poku-Spalding is an entrepreneur and women's advocate born in the UK and raised between London and Accra, Ghana.

She is the founder and CEO of The WIE Suite,[1] a membership community and platform for women leaders and creators. In addition to providing its members with the community and tools to succeed in the workplace, The WIE Suite supports brands and corporations with their culture-building and diversity initiatives. Over the years, Dee has attracted numerous business and cultural leaders to her global gatherings, including Queen Rania, Melinda Gates, Mellody Hobson, Shan-Lyn Ma, Naomi Campbell, Arianna Huffington, Thasunda Duckett, Diane von Furstenberg, Nancy Pelosi, Katia Beauchamp, Jill Biden, Jennifer Hyman, Alek Wek, Tyra Banks, Aileen Lee, Lauren Bush, Iman, Rosario Dawson, and Christy Turlington.

Back in 2010, Dee cofounded The WIE Symposium—one of the early modern women's conferences, created partly in response to the lack of diversity at traditional business forums.

Dee also founded The Other Festival, a platform for female makers and creators, and Black Women Raise, an initiative designed to increase access to capital for black female founders.

A former Hollywood studio executive, Dee's background includes senior marketing roles at Paramount Pictures and Focus Features (a division of Universal Pictures), working with the likes of Angelina Jolie, Brad Pitt, Samuel L. Jackson, Reese Witherspoon, Scarlett Johansson, Bill Murray, Emily Blunt, and Taraji P. Henson. She has worked on numerous award-winning films, including Al Gore's *An Inconvenient Truth*; the Coen brothers' *No Country for Old Men* and *O Brother, Where Art Thou?*; Sofia Coppola's *Lost in Translation*; Alejandro González Iñárritu's *Babel* and *21 Grams*; and Ang Lee's *Brokeback Mountain*.

Dee began her career in brand marketing and communications and over the years has worked with renowned brands such as Coca-Cola, Absolut Vodka, Crème de la Mer, Stella Artois, and London Fashion Week.

Dee has been named one of *Marie Claire* magazine's "50 women who are changing the world," a Council of Urban Professionals (CUP) Catalyst Changemaker, a Harlem Fashion Week Cultural Icon, and one of TRUE Africa's 100 Top Innovators. As an industry leader, she's been featured in the *New York Times*, *Women's Wear Daily*, Refinery 29, *Forbes*, MSNBC, and the *Guardian*. She is a frequent speaker on women's workplace advancement and culture and community building, and she has shared her insights at the UN, the New York Times New Rules Summit, the Women's March summit, the Black Girls Rock Summit, the Girlboss Rally, The Female Quotient, SHE Summit, the Makers Summit, the CUP Women's Leadership Forum, the Acumen Fund's New Leadership for Tomorrow, Stern's and Georgetown University's Women's Summits, and British Academy of Film and Television Arts, among others.

Dee serves on the board of directors of the British Academy of Film and Television Arts (BAFTA) and was previously on the Credit Suisse New Markets Women's Advisory Board. She is also an advisor to Girlgaze, Paint Box, the Female Founder Collective, The Wonder, and Après. She also serves as a contributor to *Forbes*. Dee holds a Bachelor of Science in math. She currently lives in New York with her husband and son.

A MUTUAL FRIEND introduced me to Dee. We met for tea on a rainy evening at a restaurant on Gold Street, near Wall Street, in downtown New York City. We spoke for hours about her immigrant experience and entrepreneurial journey. Dee's WIE Suite is a truly extraordinary community of trailblazing women who are committed to helping one another succeed and to making a massive impact in our world.

Greatness Is Within Reach

Kofi Annan, Ghanaian former secretary-general of the United Nations; Wole Soyinka, Nigerian poet, playwright, and essayist and winner of the Nobel Prize in Literature; Ellen Johnson Sirleaf, former president of Liberia and the first elected female head of state in Africa; Yaa Asantewaa, valiant Ghanaian woman who led an army that fought against British colonialism in 1900: Growing up in the UK, Dee was the only Black girl in the school, but her Ghanaian upbringing laid the foundation for who she is today. Her parents exposed her to strong role models—people who looked like her and occupied leadership roles in the world. For Dee, there were no mental barriers to success. As she noted in an August 2011 blog post in the Huffington Post titled "My Africa," "When people who look like you fill the influential roles in society, the heads of state, the judges, the doctors and the bankers, nothing feels impossible or out of reach. When the writers, television stars, artists and musicians all look like you, you simply don't know any different. This allowed me to succeed in life—and I feel lucky."

Life Across Three Continents

Dee's Ghanaian family had lived in the United Kingdom since the 1960s. In 2003, she decided to leave the UK and pursue a career in the United States. Her company moved her to their New York location.

Once in New York, Dee began to adjust to American culture, which included Americans' cut-to-the-chase approach, which was in stark contrast to the Brits' polite speaking style. Back then, her mannerisms included a double dose of niceness—a combination of British politeness and Ghanaian humility. She was quiet and self-effacing.

Dee notes that Americans are "a bit flummoxed by the British accent." People sometimes speak to her over the phone and are confounded when they meet her in person. They struggle to reconcile the Ghanaian woman in front of them with the mental picture they had formed based on her strong British accent.

Reels and Runways

Dee started out in the fashion industry. She was the first one in and the last one out of the office. She got coffee and sandwiches for senior colleagues and stuffed envelopes. She did whatever needed to be done and the tasks no one else wanted to do. She did them all with a smile. She was young, enthusiastic, and eager to succeed.

Dee worked on a couple of movies about fashion, and these led to her transition into the film industry. Each of the opportunities she's developed were as a result of relationships she leveraged along the way. Dee is a strong believer in the power of relationships.

Entrepreneurship Is No Hollywood Romance Movie

After years in Hollywood, Dee was ready for a change. She wanted to own a business and start a family. Starting her own business was terrifying. She hadn't realized how much of her professional and personal identities were tied to working for well-established companies and brands. She had always been Dee from X, Y, or Z powerhouse. Once she launched her own business, she was just Dee. She felt exposed.

Despite her background in film and fashion, Dee does not believe in glamorizing or romanticizing entrepreneurship. She offers nuts-and-bolts advice to entrepreneurs. She advises new entrepreneurs to create a financial cushion. It is tough not knowing when or where the next paycheck will come from, so new entrepreneurs should leave themselves something to go to. In the early days, she relied on her network. When Dee needed a workspace, a client gave her a desk at his company. Today, through her organization, Dee creates and shares resources that she wished were available to her as a new entrepreneur. She connects world-changing women leaders, enabling them to create even more impact through partnership and collaboration.

"No" Is Your Call to Action

Dee once met with a highly successful friend and mentor for dinner. She needed this conversation and was grateful that he'd agreed to meet with her because she had heard "no" a lot lately. Dee didn't like to hear noes. Indeed, she wasn't used to rejection. She'd previously been used to doors flinging wide open for her.

Most recently, she'd reached out to an old colleague regarding a job opportunity, and she hadn't heard back. Being ignored made Dee feel irrelevant, unimportant, small, and like a bit of a failure.

That night, she expected empathy from her dear mentor, along with, to be sure, some practical advice that she would dutifully go forth and execute.

After Dee summarized the recent events, her mentor seemed thoroughly confused. He didn't understand why Dee found rejection disempowering. As it relates to rejection, he told her, he lived by a simple principle: "When I get rejected, it spurs me on to prove them wrong. Rejection is an invitation to step up, a call to action."

Dee describes this as a transformational point in her journey. She realized that she had spent her early career "mumbling her way through things." After this conversation, she began to think more expansively. She understood that she needed to imbibe all she wanted to be. She needed to feel it to be it.

Dee also notes that there are many reasons people say no. Women tend to be more hindered by rejection. "We internalize it," she said, "but it is not always your fault. More importantly, if this one thing doesn't work out, something good will *always* come along—this is a truism. The question is, will you be prepared?"

Dee's Definition of Success

Dee's definition of success has evolved over the years. Early in her career, her idea of success was to get to the corner office with a view overlooking the city, carrying what she calls "the most relevant handbag." Today, she defines success as finding balance between being a successful businesswoman, a partner to her husband, and a great mom—and getting all three to work synergistically. She feels that her son is her one big accomplishment.

She notes that fulfilling these key roles requires discipline. We need to delegate as much as possible. If we are disciplined, we can get all the areas working well.

DEE'S IMMIGRACE

- Women's advocate
- Super connector
- Marketer for impact

DEE'S IMMIGEMS

◊ *Be open and forgiving.* Don't arrive at situations with pre-conceptions. We hold ourselves back when we see the negative and focus on it. Do not be insecure, and don't jump to conclusions, as this will prevent you from shining. Everyone has some prejudice, negative or not. We need to be forgiving in order to let our best selves—and those of others—to shine through.

◊ *Fight isolationism.* Don't do everything on your own. Dee attributes much of what she's built to her network. When she relocated to New York, she tapped into her network. She emailed everyone she knew in NYC, and this helped immensely with the transition. She's a big believer in making meaningful relationships and connecting with others.

◊ *Always have a plan, and prepare to adapt.* Dee often sees two extremes in women leaders, particularly entrepreneurs. Some jump in headfirst, with no plan at all, and others are rigid in following a particular path and don't adjust when circumstances demand it. Have a plan, but be adaptable.

13.
Seek the Impossible

NKECHI AKUNWAFOR
Certified Public Accountant
and Corporate Accounting Director

Nkechi Akunwafor is a certified public accountant (CPA) and a director of corporate accounting at PVH Corp., a clothing company that owns brands such as Van Heusen, Tommy Hilfiger, and Calvin Klein. She began her career as an auditor at Ernst & Young, and she moved on from there to become a finance manager at Colgate Palmolive, where she worked from 2004 to 2014. She began at Colgate as a financial analyst and steadily rose through the ranks.

NKECHI AND I have been friends for years. Our children are peers. I first met Nkechi at my son's baptism in 2005. Her childhood friend and quasi-cousin Nnedi (also profiled in this book) and I were roommates in law school. What has surprised me in the process of writing this book is that there was an entire chunk of Nkechi's journey to becoming who she is today that I didn't know about. By the time she and I became friends, she'd overcome so much. I am grateful that this project offered me the opportunity to hear her inspiring story.

A Tale of Three Aunts

Every immigrant minor who relocates to the United States without their parents likely has an aunt, uncle, or family-friend story. These adult guardians temporarily assume parental responsibilities. Their characters range from saintly to horrific. They could be featured on a religious television spotlight on the saints among us or the paranormal channel. In any event, they form a critical part of the journey.

Nkechi's guardians were her aunts. The first chapter in the "aunties saga" began when Nkechi was seventeen, fresh off the plane, when she migrated to the United States after high school. Her parents knew their children could benefit from the many opportunities in the United States, particularly education. After some soul searching, they shipped off the eldest of their four children to live with Aunt Number One in Nashville, Tennessee. Nkechi was a trailblazer, paving the way for her siblings, who eventually migrated to the United States as well.

Nkechi lived in Nashville for nine months, babysitting her aunt's three kids and receiving a small allowance, approximately twenty dollars per week. And no, it wasn't a lot of money, even in the mid-1990s. Your average McDonald's employee at the time earned twenty dollars in four hours.

It was a cycle of kids' mess: Clean. More mess. Clean again. Pretty soon, Nkechi was bored with this, and not to mention mildly irritated. So she got a job as a cashier at a grocery store. Because Nkechi's mom owned a store while Nkechi was growing up in Nigeria, working at a grocery store was somewhat familiar territory.

One fateful day, the family threw a party. Her aunt asked her to clean up after the guests had departed. Something about the way Nkechi responded made her aunt feel disrespected, and a disagreement ensued. Nkechi apparently didn't behave like the "well-brought-up child" her aunt thought she was supposed to be.

This marked the end of Nkechi's days in Nashville.

Nkechi then went to live with Aunt Number Two in New Jersey. It was time to begin her education. She enrolled in the same community college her aunt attended; it was the convenient option. For many immigrants, initial choices are often determined by the choices made by those closest to us (relatives and friends), whether or not such individuals are living the American Dream as we'd like to define it for ourselves. Critical to the success of the women profiled in this book is their ability to break away from limited choices, tap into their immigrace, and embrace the unlimited possibilities here in the United States.

Nkechi's aunt was newly married and continually engaged in altercations with her husband. From her bedroom, Nkechi would hear them curse each other out, using the vilest words. Nkechi would sit in her room, wondering when it would end. She would wake up, get dressed for the day, and get out, and when she returned home she would hide out in her room. She also couldn't have visitors. A neighbor once came to visit and faced a veritable firing squad. So Nkechi had to meet her friends outside the house.

Then the animosity between her aunt and her aunt's husband began to spread to her. She would call home and beg to move. Her prayers were answered when she moved in with Aunt Number Three.

Aunt Number Three was a bit of a saint, a true gem. They got along beautifully. But eventually, auntie-the-saint decided to move back to Nigeria.

Big-Girl Boots

It was time for Nkechi to put on her big-girl boots and get her own place. At this point, she had been in the United States for about a year and a half. She got an apartment in Brooklyn, conveniently next door to her aunt's old place. Very quickly, she was living the joys of water and electricity bills, rent, and supporting herself. She was still a teenager. She had two jobs, as an office assistant at a law firm and as a sales associate at an American Eagle Outfitters retail store. Growing up in Nigeria, she would never have thought that she would need to be self-sufficient at eighteen years old.

Soon, her younger sister, Ayesha ("Aye"), joined her in the United States. Aye had big dreams. She wanted to go to a *real* university, as she described it, not a community college. By now, Nkechi was wrapping up community college, so the two studied together for the SATs.

Aye was home and looking for a job in the period before starting school. Although Nkechi was working two jobs, they realized that they never seemed to have enough money to pay the rent for their one-bedroom, quasi-studio Brooklyn apartment. They often ate ramen noodles for dinner.

Whenever the rent was past due, Aye would call Nkechi at the law firm. Heart pounding and whispering, Aye would tell her that their seventy-year-old landlord was, once again, pounding on the door with his walking stick. Nkechi would advise Aye not to open the door. They would call their mom and dad, who faithfully wired money to pay the past-due rent. "We are dying!" they would declare to their parents. "They are going to put us out on the street!"

People often think of remittances going from the United States to the developing world. What many do not realize is that, quite often, the immigrant struggle in the United States is so dire that the requests come from the States and the money flows from the developing world to the States.

In another unusual reversal, when Nkechi's sister moved out to attend college, one of their aunts moved in with nineteen-year-old Nkechi. This was the aunt who repeatedly fought with her husband. She was going through a difficult divorce and transition and was between homes. Auntie promised to help pay the bills, and Nkechi welcomed the offer with arms as wide open as the Atlantic Ocean.

In the midst of a heated argument with this aunt—Nkechi does not recall the precise cause or subject of this disagreement—her aunt declared, "You will never make more than $50,000 a year."

When one challenges you with limiting beliefs, it is time to set your goal well beyond what you think is possible and aim for the stars. From within, Nkechi felt a sense of defiance, as though she had been dared: *I'm not settling for par*, she thought. *I'm shooting for stars.* Looking back, Nkechi is convinced that this was a turning point in her life. Her aunt's statement cast her onto a path of becoming who she is today. She resolved to go to a four-year college, become an accountant, and earn no less than $50,000 a year. She has since surpassed these goals, but what's most instructive about this is that she made a firm decision in that moment and began to align her actions with her goals.

Nkechi studied hard for the SATs and was admitted to Binghamton University. She moved out of the apartment and into the dorms.

The Wait-a-Minute Moment

Because Nkechi got straight As in community college, she took college for granted. She had become a certified nurse aid and worked two jobs to support herself.

She had a rather impolite awakening when her grade point average fell below 2.0 and she was placed on academic probation. She paid the school counselor a visit. "What does this mean?" she asked. The counselor's answers to that question led to a "wait-a-damn-minute" moment. If she continued down the path she was on, she would never attain her goal of being a CPA. She wasn't ready to let go of that dream.

The Hustle

Nkechi found web discussion groups about accounting and spent time devouring all the nuggets on the sites. She spent hours at the library consuming much of the same kind of information. The counselor helped her polish her résumé.

She resolved to ace every single exam over the next two semesters, and she studied like her life depended on it.

Her next challenge was landing an internship during her junior year. Because she had transferred to the university during the second semester of her sophomore year, most of her peers were already well into the process of completing all the prerequisites for an internship. She did not let this deter her but continued to network aggressively in her last two years of college. She asked everyone who did get an internship to introduce her to their recruiters. She raised her GPA in her major to a 4.0, such that her guidance counselor advised that she put her major GPA on her résumé, highlighting for potential employers her commitment and abilities specific to the field.

She joined various student organizations, such as the National Association of Black Accountants (NABA). It was at an NABA convention during her final year of college that she met her husband, Obi.

When it was time to interview for postcollege jobs, Nkechi was prepared. She maintained a 4.0 GPA in her major. What sealed the deal for her? She told her story about coming to the United States alone at seventeen years old, struggling her way through aunts and electric bills. Interviewers sensed her remarkable drive. Once again, it proved that one of the very things that some immigrants seek to shy away from, hide, or minimize is their biggest asset: their immigrant story.

By her senior year, Nkechi secured offers from four of what were then known as the Big Five accounting firms. These firms offered her $60,000 as a starting annual salary. She picked Ernst & Young (E&Y), and so began her professional journey. All of the other members of their incoming class had interned at E&Y the prior summer. Nkechi was the exception, as she received a full-time offer without an internship.

Shooting for the Stars

Nkechi became a CPA, and after almost three years at E&Y, she transitioned to Colgate Palmolive. She had only been at Colgate for a year when a senior analyst on her team left. She was asked to take on the analyst's role. One of her colleagues, who had been on the team longer than Nkechi, expected to be the logical choice. She had been in same role for five years and had not been promoted. Nkechi believes her colleague had become complacent in the role.

Within seven years, Nkechi served in five different roles. In almost every instance, she was tapped for a new position with more responsibilities. In one instance, she asked for it, and the hiring manager told her he had been hoping she would ask.

While reflecting on the reasons she'd steadily risen in the company, Nkechi noted that from her first day at the company, she was highly curious, took initiative, spoke up, asked questions, and built relationships. She sought to understand the context for her tasks, and, whether she loved it or hated it, she always had a view. You could be the president of the United States, but if she had a problem, you'd hear about it and you would hear why.

After looking back on her initial years of struggle, Nkechi says she would have it no other way; the experiences all helped build her character. She strongly believes that life is what you make it: Each of us is the driver on our journey through life. Every struggle is a bump in the road. We can choose to let struggles bring us down, or they can make us stronger. Every day, Nkechi choses the latter. Whatever happens, she says, buckle up and get back on the road.

Nkechi's Definition of Success

Success is attaining the goals you have set for yourself and the achievements you've aspired to, both in the short term and in the long term. Success is manifesting and living your dreams and daydreams (even the ones that are true pipe dreams). Success is being able to account for all the hard work, perseverance, and noes that got you to your goal. Success means never giving up . . . it's at the end of that tunnel.

NKECHI'S IMMIGRACE

- Extraordinary certified public accountant, corporate director, and leader

NKECHI'S IMMIGEMS

◇ *Have a positive attitude.* There is always a positive. Your challenge is to find it and not ignore it. You cannot get ahead as a Debbie Downer.

◇ *Have a sense of humor.* Just as important as finding the positive is finding humor in situations. Humor is therapeutic—tap into it.

◇ *Take initiative.* Even if you were raised in a culture in which you were accustomed to being told what to do, you have to step out of that and figure out what is required to succeed in your chosen endeavor. Do what is required, and persevere at it—every single day.

Immigrace Journal

1. What are three major life experiences I've defined as failures?

    _____

    _____

    _____

2. What lessons did I take from those experiences?

    _____

    _____

    _____

3. What role have they played in my journey?

    _____

    _____

    _____

4. How can I grow through them?

    _____

    _____

    _____

5. How can I use my "why" to reframe those experiences?

    _____

    _____

    _____

PART V
Embrace Change and Innovate

The immigrace journey demands ongoing transformation. As long as we are alive, the journey is never done. If you love comfort, you will never live fulfillment. This is not because we are aiming for some unattainable success or because we are never satisfied. It's because we are fully committed to this journey called life. It's because our purpose can evolve, from giving to learning, from learning to serving, and from serving to seeking out new skills. Life supports change, growth, and evolution.

Embrace Change by Embracing Discomfort

Greek philosopher Heraclitus famously said: "nothing is permanent except change."

The material world around us is continually undergoing transformation. The weather changes and seasons change. The stars go through the cycle from giant gas cloud to supernovae and planetary nebulae. All human beings go through a life cycle of birth, growth, and death.

Yet, humans resist change in part because of our need for certainty. We value security, stability, predictability, and reliability. Paradoxically, another one of our human needs is uncertainty or variety. We would get bored without some degree of variety in our lives and need to vary our emotions, environments, and activities.

Our human needs are not of themselves good or bad, what matters is how we fulfill those needs, whether we do so in ways that are optimal and empowering to ourselves and those around us, or if we do it in ways that are disempowering. How highly we value these needs determines the extent to which we pursue them.

Despite our inclinations to resist change, we know that life is ever evolving, and people and things continually change states, whether or not such change is visible.

Better yet, we should force change on ourselves, so that when discomfort comes, we don't run from it. One way of forcing change on ourselves is by willingly, intentionally, and voluntarily embracing discomfort. This helps build mental strength and fortitude that helps us navigate the discomforts that are sure to come in life. It's a key principle of optimal performance, with examples ranging from monks who embrace fasting to athletes who train by following strict eating and exercise regimens.

One example I've integrated into my daily life for almost three years is the practice of taking cold showers. The practice involves taking a shower at the usual temperature, but switching to the coldest temperature for at least sixty seconds. Studies have suggested that cold water immersion contributes to the body's natural healing, including improving our immune, lymphatic, circulatory, and digestive systems, and reducing muscle inflammation. It wakes your body up and increases mental alertness.

Even as a daily habit I've practiced for years, once in a while, my brain tries to talk me out of it. Herein lies one of our greatest powers—the power to override the brain, and the stories it generates. In sticking to the intention and overriding the brain's suggestion to take the easier path, I train my brain to understand that I always have the ability to live with intention and purpose.

Why Innovate?

Creation, innovation, and invention are close relatives that summarize the ideas in this section. These are some of the most important acts we can engage in as human beings. We are continually creating. Part of the problem is that, as discussed in Part II in relation to habits, we don't always do so consciously or intentionally. And hence, we may often create more of what we don't want.

To intentionally put a mark on the world by introducing something that wasn't previously in it or by substantially improving something that was, that is the work of creation, innovation, and invention.

Margaret Boden, author of *The Creative Mind: Myths and Mechanisms* defines Creativity as "the ability to come up with ideas or artifacts that are new, surprising, and valuable."[1]

We should put our own unique mark on the world because it's why we are here. It is why each of us is endowed with unique gifts, interests, passions, and journeys. Creativity not only contributes to the world, but also contributes to our happiness. Creativity takes decision, commitment, and consistent investment of time and focus, in order to move from endowed talents and inclinations to mastery.

Immigrants and Innovation

The United States, as the greatest experiment in the history of mankind, continues to attract large populations of immigrants who arrive with big dreams and aspirations. Researchers have long been fascinated by immigrants' successes in the United States and several volumes have been dedicated to understanding it.

Eric Weiner, author of *The Geography of Genius: A Search for the World's Most Creative Places, From Ancient Athens to Silicon Valley,* noted in a 2016 Wall Street Journal article that "Having your world turned upside down sparks creative thinking." He intimated that immigrants surpass the merely talented in large part due to their "oblique perspective . . . uprooted from the familiar, they see the world at an angle." Immigrants also possess "openness to experience," observing that such openness often sparks ingenuity in entire societies where cultural influxes occur. However, he also acknowledges that not all cultural collisions end well and that not all "immigrants become geniuses."[2]

Since being an immigrant doesn't automatically guarantee genius status, you're probably wondering how to ignite your own creative genius. I told you in Part I that I'm not a fan of mysterious and unapproachable ideas. The *how* of sparking creativity, innovation, and invention is therefore simple. Simple, but not easy.

Here are seven mutually reinforcing rules of creativity:

GET QUIET

Regular practice of quiet time is a discipline and requires the intentional elimination of distractions. Ways to get quiet vary, each with their own unique benefits, so the intention is not to conflate them, but to underscore that each of them independently and jointly contribute to a creative life. Meditation, contemplative or mental prayer, quiet time, and thinking time are all examples of getting quiet.

These were particularly difficult habits for me to entrench for two reasons. First, I'm an extrovert. I am refueled by engaging and interacting with others. I've been known to arrive home from twenty-hour-long international flights from business trips to Asia, and to the astonishment of my introverted husband, still joyfully attend social commitments, such as award events or other celebratory events, without first catching up on sleep. Equally surprising were times I would wrap up marathon conference calls, beginning at 7:00 a.m. and ending at 7:00 p.m., yet still being excited about taking our youngest to the Boy Scouts' outing or joining my girl-friends for a boat cruise on Lake Mohawk. After over fifteen years of marriage, my husband finds these far less confounding, just as conversely, I've learned to better understand his inclination to-ward introversion.

The second reason getting quiet was challenging for me to adopt is that I have an active personality. As a toddler, I was accustomed to climbing and breaking things. If you know me today, you'd probably agree that these traits are not very far. I earned a scar on my right cheek from climbing a pavement at home during a birthday party. The cele-bration was disrupted when I had to be rushed to the nearest hospital. My mom was in a panic because the cuts were close to my left eye, and they feared that something got in my eye and would ultimately impair my vision. As the family legend goes, all was well when I emerged from the theater with stitches, cracking jokes with the physician.

I tell you this to emphasize that I am not one who is naturally in-clined to sitting still. It is a habit that I have adopted and cultivated over time through practice because studies have repeatedly demon-strated the benefits of getting quiet (such as mental clarity, reduc-tion of depression, and increased productivity), but perhaps more importantly, the results I've experienced in my own life—living my purpose and accomplishing seemingly extraordinary feats that have far exceeded any specific goals I've set.

Contemplative or mental prayer is a meditative practice of get-ting quiet with God, entering into an intimate dialogue, being open, and listening. I prioritize contemplative prayer over all other forms of getting quiet.

Getting quiet is not only beneficial as a spiritual practice, but it is also a sound business practice. Trevor Blake, author of *Three Simple Steps: A Map to Success in Business and Life*, recommends the prac-tice of sitting quietly for twenty minutes every day, journaling your intentions (as if they have already come to pass), and spending time immersed in nature, as essential tools for success.

In addition, I've described Keith Cunningham's book, *The Road Less Stupid: Advice from the Chairman of the Board* as one of the best business books ever written. In it, he strongly advocates the practice of thinking time, which involves spending thirty to forty-five minutes in uninterrupted concentration. The process requires advance preparation of a high value question. The better the question, the more insightful and robust the answers. Thinking time questions revolve around the following principles: find the unasked question; separate the problem from the symptom; check assumptions; consider second order consequences (risks and possibility of being wrong); and create the machine (executable plan). I've applied Keith's process in a number of scenarios and highly recommend it to business leaders and entrepreneurs.

WANDER

Genius writers through history, including Maya Angelou, Henry David Thoreau, and Ernest Hemingway, to mention a few, have lauded the importance of nature walks and wandering aimlessly. Researchers at Stanford University also found that walking boosts creative output by 60 percent. In seeking to understand the remarkable connection between walking and innovation, researchers have pointed to a few possible explanations, including: (1) Exercise is good for the brain; (2) Walking, in particular, leverages multiple parts of the brain—the left and right sides of the neocortex associated with logical/linear and creativity/intuition respectively. In walking, we continually shift from the left to the right, including with our feet, thereby increasing communication between both sides of the brain; and (3) Walking offers cognitive pause and the ability to offload, in order to make room for new ideas.[3]

STAY CURIOUS

Curiosity is a powerful state of mind because it is a state of openness, learning, and it is ultimately indispensable in the process of innovation. Children are curious and this supports their strong imagination which also leads to higher levels of creativity. Adults undermine their creative inclinations by believing they have all the answers and therefore don't open themselves up to learning new things. Nurture your sense of wonder by asking questions, noticing changes around you, and drawing connections. Be willing to try out new ideas, new and different ways of doing things, and allowing for failure. Take a new route to work. Wear your hair differently for a week. Wear a color you typically wouldn't wear. Explore a new shade of lipstick.

INTEGRATE PLAY INTO YOUR WORK AND LIFE

Play is one of the most underappreciated tools for creativity and success. Similar to how society urges us to discard curiosity as adults, the same is the case for play. Yet, research has repeatedly shown that integrating fun into our adult lives can help us realize some of the intentions that are most important to us. Greg McKeown notes the importance of play in enriching our creative capacities and expanding our horizons to come up with new ideas.[4]

My team at work has integrated practices such as these to integrate play into work, and I find that these practices are not only uplifting, but also increase our productivity: color or hat themed days, crafts, team *Jeopardy!* days, decorating the workplace, and celebrating accomplishments throughout the day, including celebrating small milestones.

In life, you can integrate play on a regular basis by playing card or board games with children; adopting a hobby involving a fun physical activity such as dance or a sport; or coloring and sketching. Be sure to select fun activities—resist the temptation to embark on challenging feats. Fun is the primary goal here.

HONE YOUR INTUITION AND TRUST IT

One of the greatest flaws of the modern workplace is an overemphasis on male traits and attributes. The highest levels in a lot of industries are heavily dominated by men because traits more predominantly demonstrated by men are highly valued and considered to be essential to success.

Scientists define intuition as our brain's ability to draw on internal and external cues in making rapid, in-the-moment decisions. Usually occurring outside of our conscious awareness, intuition relies on our brain's ability to instantaneously evaluate both internal and external cues, and make a decision based on what appears to be pure instinct.

Research has found that intuition is the result of the way our brains store, process, and retrieve information.

A study compared male and female brain connectivity using MRI scans and discovered that the typical male brain is neurologically wired to be more logical, and thus is more effective at linking perception with action.[4] Although both men and women have the capacity for intuition, women's brains are more hardwired for it.

Even setting aside the brain research, consider how frequently traits such as the ability to listen to one's intuition are downplayed, ignored, or discouraged in business and in the workplace. The logical, fact-based argument is prioritized over intuition.

There are other traits that are similarly situated, and these include empathy, understanding, sharing, and nurturing. Doing is also prioritized over being. Paradoxes, which are seemingly illogical on the surface, are quickly ignored or dismissed in a rush to the next obvious, big idea. Solid, structured, disciplined, protective, steady, linear, analytical attributes are valued over creative, changing, flowing, non-linear, and evolving attributes. The overemphasis on certain traits leads to distortions in the workplace, and in my view, decreased efficiency, suboptimal results, and often, burnout.

To be clear, men and women posess all of these attributes, but the differences lie in the inclinations. Similarly, men and women can sharpen their intuition and increase the practice of listening to it. Two of my male mentors intentionally and consistently prioritize empathy and understanding as core values, and this makes them the most highly effective leaders I've encountered in my life.

Masculine and feminine traits should be properly understood in order to create harmony and optimally efficient and productive workplaces that serve individuals and society, a critical priority in the post-COVID pandemic workplace. Properly leveraging the various traits and inclinations would lead to results that are rarely, if ever, tapped into.

Most importantly, for purposes of this discussion on innovation, my advice to female warriors is: your intuition is priceless, and you should never, under any circumstances, dismiss, ignore, or disregard it in order to advance in the workplace. If you nurture, hone, and listen to your intuition, it will be one of your greatest assets in life and business.

RECORD YOUR BRILLIANT IDEAS

Brilliant ideas come to us hundreds of times throughout the day. If you frequently spend time in silence, their frequency and volume will exponentially increase. As you notice things around you, take note of them. Your task is to ensure that you do not let them evaporate, or move through you like passing winds and on to the next thing. Grab onto them, record them, and choose which ideas you want to dedicate time and effort to bringing to life through research, exploration, and iteration.

FOLLOW THE PATH

This is the process of researching, exploring, iterating, and ultimately bringing your brilliant idea to life. Use the intention and goal setting process in part III to follow the path. Taking steps toward executing your idea brings more clarity, understanding, and opportunities to refine your product, service, or solution. Remember that the path is not only to the delivery of a particular end goal or reaching a destination, it is the path to the full realization of who you are, through the participation in the creative process.

IN THIS SECTION, you'll meet three women who share how they navigated important transition points in their lives and careers; and how they continually grow, learn, and lead:

- Sasha Grinshpun, executive coach, career architect, facilitator, thought leader, strategist, and design-thinking practitioner. Russia-born Sasha shares the story of discrimination against Jews in Russia, being part of the Refusenik movement, her family's exodus to the United States, and her views about certain limiting immigrant beliefs and mindsets.

- Laura Giradorou Koch, founder and CEO of Women 4 Solutions, Inc., system social entrepreneur, caring economy advocate, philanthropist, innovative educator, board member for NGO and corporations, and attorney. Argentina-born to Italian immigrants, Laura relocated to the United States to obtain a law degree. She penned a controversial article challenging corruption in Argentina in the 1980s. A dyslexic, she now commits to philanthropy, innovative education, and inspires students and others to social entrepreneurship around the world.

- Adela Williams, talent-acquisition strategist. Born in Peru to a Peruvian mother and Italian-American father, Adela relocated to the United States when she was five years old. Growing up in the melting pot of Newark, NJ in the 1980s and in serving as an executive recruiter, she has learned the importance of diversity in the workplace, and overcoming unconscious bias to find talented people with passion and purpose.

- Ugo Ukabam; labor and employment lawyer and senior counsel at General Mills, Inc. Nigeria-born Ugo was the first racial minority female to achieve partner status in a large Minneapolis law firm. Hers is a story of navigating law school as a single mom of two and experiencing discrimination in Minnesota and being an advocate for change.

14.
What Do You Really Want?

SASHA GRINSHPUN

Executive Coach, Career Architect,
Facilitator, Thought Leader, Strategist,
and Design-Thinking Practitioner

Sasha Grinshpun consults with Fortune 1000 companies looking to revamp, strengthen, or define their global human capital strategy. With clients including Harvard, Yale, Google, and Yahoo!, Sasha has delivered high-impact projects and workshops spanning the topics of career development, leadership development, the multigenerational workforce, and work-life management. Sought after as a strategic talent-management expert, Sasha has been featured in such prominent news forums as NPR and the *Washington Post*.

For professionals, Sasha combines her gift for quickly gauging life passions of her clients with her experience in formulating effective job searches for them to sculpt their dream jobs. Her eclectic background spanning consulting, IDEO, and entrepreneurial ventures puts her in a unique position to have conversations around the question "What do you really want?"

For young adults, Sasha helps students navigate the fraught college-admissions and undergraduate journey. She helps her clients consider their full selves, including skills, motivators, and deep interests, to help craft internship programs and a networking strategy that are the basis of agile career planning.

Sasha is a sought-after public and keynote speaker on topics including networking, career visioning, and personal branding. Speaking engagements span alumni associations, global professional organizations, and conferences.

Throughout any engagement, Sasha combines empathy, strategic insight, and design thinking to help clients achieve breakthroughs.

In addition to her background in business, Sasha conducted genetic research as part of the Human Genome Project and wrote documentary scripts for National Geographic Television.

Sasha graduated from Harvard Business School, at which she launched Career Teams, a campus-wide job-mentoring program. Before Harvard, she received a BA in economics and international studies from Yale, where she also developed an addiction to learning languages. Fluent in Russian, Portuguese, and Spanish, Sasha is now learning Mandarin and relearning French. She lives in the San Francisco Bay Area with her family.

WHEN SASHA AND I spoke over the phone several years ago, she told me that as she lounged on her deck the weather was so incredibly beautiful in sunny Northern California that she had to pinch herself.

We exchanged common memories of Harvard (hers from the business school and mine from the law school). Sasha remains active in the Harvard Business School alumni community in the San Francisco Bay area. Each time we speak, I'm struck by how beautifully Sasha combines her design thinking wisdom with a sense of humor, warmth, wit, and grace.

Refusenik:
Solidarity, Struggle, and Liberation

"Why would I waste a perfectly good spot on a Jew?"

The dean of Moscow State University posed this question to Sasha's aunt. Sasha's cousin was a mathematical genius, so, understandably, he applied to the very best school he knew—Moscow State University, which was the Harvard University equivalent in the Soviet Union at the time. The problem was that Soviet Jews were not allowed access to the best things.

Living in Ukraine under the Soviet Communist regime in the early 1970s, Sasha's family experienced blatant and subtle forms of discrimination. The "waste of a perfectly good spot" question was prototypical. Unable to rise within society, Jews couldn't lead institutions and could only occupy positions as middle managers or below. They were unable to practice their religion freely, but were also unable to leave the Soviet Union.

Let's briefly explore the history of Jews in the Soviet Union. The Soviet Union emerged as a Communist country in 1922, following several bloody wars and revolutions. As the Soviet Union continued to consolidate power, and through the takeover of Poland, the Baltic states, and Romania, the population of Jews in the Soviet Union grew from approximately three million in 1922 to five million in 1939. Soviet authorities worked toward the elimination of all organized religion, with the ultimate goal of establishing state atheism. Observers of various religions—Jews, Catholics, Russian Orthodox, Baptists, and Protestants—were targeted. The tools of intimidation included property confiscation, imprisonment, and the murder of religious leaders.

In 1941, the Nazis invaded the Soviet Union. In addition to the military, the Nazis utilized mobile killing units, *Einsatzgruppen*, to eliminate the Jewish population. The Nazis massacred 30 million people, including 2.5 million Jews.

Following the death of Stalin in 1953, there was a Jewish revival in the Soviet Union. And in 1967, following the Six-Day War, there was, once again, an awakening of Jewish consciousness in the Soviet Union. However, injustices persisted for Soviet Jews.

Refusenik, or *отказник* in Russian, had its origins in a term that was used to describe Soviet authorities' denial of requests to leave the Soviet Union. Applicants who sought to leave the country but remained in the Soviet Union were in a state of "refusal" and were referred to as Refuseniks. Refuseniks were treated as enemies of the state. They lost their homes or jobs and were subjected to state police surveillance, bullying, and harassment.

Refusenik became much more than the description of a status of one whose immigration request had been denied. It evolved into one of the most powerful freedom movements of the twentieth century.

Refuseniks covertly built their Jewish culture by teaching Hebrew and practicing religious and cultural traditions. Importantly, however, Refuseniks also overtly challenged the state through various forms of protest, including the distribution of materials and articles in the media to document the injustices and harassment they experienced. By the 1970s, there was growing international support for the Refusenik movement. Jews in the United States held candlelight vigils and marches in support for their sisters and brothers behind the Iron Curtain. They also pushed for various American policies, including immigration policies, to support Soviet Jews. For the courageous Jews who lived in the Soviet Union, however, the consequences of protest were increasingly severe—imprisonment, sham trials, and death.

Mikhail Gorbachev, the eighth and final leader of the Soviet Union, was general secretary of the Communist Party of the Soviet Union from 1985 to 1991 and was the country's head of state from 1988 to 1991. Gorbachev had the foresight to understand that the state of affairs in the Soviet Union was unsustainable. Under his leadership, laws that allowed for greater freedom of speech and economic freedom were passed. Activists were released from prison, large numbers of Refusenik cases were reviewed, and exit visas were issued. The Soviet Union collapsed in 1991.

It was in 1978 that Sasha's father had traveled from Ukraine to Russia to see his cousin and that she shared the story of her son's rejection from Moscow State University. That day, Sasha's father realized that his children, brilliant and talented as they were, would not have the opportunity to reach their fullest potential in the Soviet Union, and this prompted the family's decision to leave the country. They applied right away for a visa to leave.

The decision to leave was not one the family made lightly. Sasha notes that her parents were "not big into change." Applying for a visa implied big changes—instantly losing your job and a marked increase in police surveillance. The longer it took for the visa to be processed, the more dangerous and precarious it was to remain in the Soviet Union.

Leaving the Soviet Union

The family was fortunate to have their visa processed in exactly six weeks. They boarded a train to Chop, Ukraine, a border city between Ukraine and Poland, and from there they headed to Austria.

As soon as they left the Soviet Union, they were capitalists, Sasha shared, only half joking. It was in Austria that they obtained currency for their travels. They carried boxes of caviar and *matryoshka* dolls (Russian nesting dolls). They sold these in Austria—the stuff of mutual delight to Sasha's family and the tourist buyers. This was how Sasha celebrated her birthday.

When they left Austria, they spent three months in Italy, hosted by generous Italian families. Most immigrant Russian Jews obtained visas to Israel. In Rome, one could swap out the Israeli visa for an American one. If one had a family in the United States, they could sponsor you.

Immigrant Resourcefulness

The family was part of an orchestrated exodus, and a number of organizations assisted the family with the transition from the Soviet Union to the United States. For two months, Sasha's family of eight lived in the back half of a rat-infested, run-down hotel room in Brooklyn, surrounded by other Russian immigrant families. The locks didn't work. Sasha's teacher solicited clothes for her from her classmates. The family also often acquired their belongings and daily needs from the streets. Sasha vividly recalls the acquisition of a certain barely-white couch from the street. It was badly worn and ripped, so they duct-taped it. It was immigrant resourcefulness at its finest—the can-do attitude that makes the most of circumstances and resources.

The not-so-great immigrant attitude is the "must do" or "have to do" attitude and linear thinking. Sasha considers this one of the challenges she's had to overcome as an immigrant—the mentality that says, "I've got to." It's also the mentality that leads a lot of immigrants to be rigid workaholics, rather than focusing on true fulfillment.

Embracing Change

Sasha attended PS 220 and JHS 157, which she describes as being literally on the wrong side of the tracks, off Highway 495 in Queens, New York. It was a tough environment—there were bullies, fights, and incorrigible teenagers who talked back at their teachers.

While a family may migrate together, each individual family member can have radically different experiences. Sasha loves and embraces change. She contrasts this with the experiences of her mother and sister. Immigration was tough on Sasha's mom, personally and professionally. Her mom came from a large, close-knit family, so she missed them dearly. For them, as with most cultures around the world, the nuclear family is simply a fraction of who is considered family. Sasha's mom was one of twenty-five cousins and a bit of a mother hen to the extended family. The separation from family back in the Soviet Union weighed heavily on Sasha's mom.

As part of the exodus, the men (who were usually fathers) were trained, and this positively impacted their job prospects. Women and mothers were not trained. Sasha's mom was an economist back in Russia, but she ended up doing low-level bookkeeping in the United States, becoming a shadow of what she was capable of. She sacrificed her career so that her children could have a better life and so her family could be free. Sasha saw how hard this was for her mom.

Sacrifice begets gratitude. Her parents' sacrifice led to an implicit promise: "You gave up your career, success, comfort, and family, so I, in turn, will make something bigger out of this. I will do whatever it takes to make something bigger out of this."

Coming to the United States was also tough on Sasha's sister, who was eleven years old when they arrived and who left many friendships at home. Sasha's sister's friends in the United States were Russian. In contrast, all of Sasha's friends were American. Sasha quickly learned English and became the family translator. Her ability to blend in and venture into American culture empowered her.

Global Souls

Although Sasha has the ability to adapt quickly to new environments, she notes that one of the interesting things about being an immigrant is that you never truly feel like you belong. You somehow feel like a stranger in a strange land. When she lived and worked as a consultant in Brazil for four years, she spoke Portuguese and created PowerPoint presentations in Portuguese, but she never felt Brazilian. She feels the same way in the United States—as adapted as she is, she never truly feels American. She does feel at home with "global souls," as she calls them. These are often immigrants, but they're not necessarily immigrants—they are anyone who can intimately relate to being a stranger in a strange land. Not as a tourist, but as a resident who lives somewhere new, who buys groceries there and goes to the doctor. There's something profound about that process of living and adjusting to a different country. These are the people she understands and who understand her. Maybe that, in a sense, is American, but Sasha knows she can find those souls wherever she goes, and in those moments, she feels at home.

Sasha's Definition of Success

As the title of this chapter suggests, Sasha believes in asking powerful, life-defining questions. Her definition of success begins with a powerful question: At the end of this life, how do I know that I led the life I wanted to lead and that I lived it with deep meaning?

Sasha believes in challenging career-focused definitions of success. Meaning is the defining question. Viewing the definition of success outside of the realm of work helps you focus on fulfilling your purpose and cultivating meaning, whether it's through raising children, being a wife, or whatever it is that truly fulfills you.

SASHA'S IMMIGRACE

- Human and business-potential visionary and architect
- Thought leader
- Design-thinking practitioner

SASHA'S IMMIGEMS

◊ *Have a growth mindset.* In the Soviet Union, Soviet Jews' choices were limited to traditional careers, and this limited people's dreams as well. Individuals tended to be rigid workaholics who provided for their families. This was largely consistent with the fixed mindset. In the book *Mindset: The New Psychology of Success*, Carol Dweck distinguishes between the fixed mindset and the growth mindset. The two mindsets may be viewed as nonlearners and learners. Those with fixed mindsets believe in perfection right away. They believe you either have it or you do not. Those with a growth mindset understand that becoming is better than being, they embrace every experience as an opportunity to learn, and they seek out opportunities to continually improve.

Many immigrant families exemplify the fixed mindset. Perhaps you scored 98 percent on the test, but you dreaded going home because you inevitably faced the inquiry, "Where are the other two points?" It is the idea that one always has to take first place at everything one embarks upon. This approach is often applauded and associated with high achievement. Sasha challenges this. She says, "What if that's not who you were meant to be? You may be surrounded by people who embrace the fixed mindset, but in order to truly find happiness, you must challenge this. You must create your own vision and set out on the path toward that vision."

◇ *Define what self-actualization looks like for you.* In his hierarchy of needs, psychologist Abraham Maslow places the various human needs in a hierarchy, beginning with physiological needs such as air, water, food, and shelter; then moving to safety needs such as personal security, employment, and health; then moving to love and belonging such as friendship, intimacy, and family; then moving to esteem, which includes respect, status, and recognition; and finally reaching self-actualization, which is the highest level in the hierarchy and represents personal growth, self-fulfillment, and the realization of one's potential. Define what this looks like for you and live it.

◊ *Remember that immigrant women are capable of anything.* We can do anything and break down barriers because, in a sense, the immigration experience breaks you down, and that's a strength you can always tap into.

15.
Transformational Leadership

LAURA GIADOROU KOCH
Founder and CEO of Women 4 Solutions, Inc.,
System Social Entrepreneur, Caring Economy Advocate,
Philanthropist, Innovative Educator, Board Member for
NGO and Corporations, and Attorney

Laura Giadorou Koch is a system social entrepreneur, a creative changemaker and disruptor on gender parity, an advocate and practitioner on regenerative and inclusive businesses, a passionate and effective impact investor, a philanthropist, an educator on empathy skills, and a lawyer (licensed in New York State and Argentina). For over three decades, she has focused on positive impact on gender parity, microfinance, innovation technologies, and social emotional education, and she has been an advocate on climate issues.

As founder and CEO of Women 4 Solutions, she endeavors to transform the mindsets and actions of women and men globally, based on the "Caring Economy."[1] The Caring Economy consists of these four pillars: (1) the care of the environment, (2) the "Work of Care," (3) high-quality early childhood education and reskilling, and (4) transparency and metrics on the Caring Economy.

Through Women 4 Solutions, Laura is living her life purpose: "to create awareness and inspire action for people and institutions toward a Caring Economy," she says. With her team of many volunteers globally, she organizes hundreds of webinars, workshops, and certifications, focusing on the four pillars of the Caring Economy. Women 4 Solutions prides itself on delivering simple, practical, and effective tools for personal growth and professional excellence.

For over two decades, Laura has been the CEO of Dolium Bodega Subterranea, a winery in Mendoza, Argentina, and the first winery in Latin America to qualify for the B Corp certification given by B Lab, which also named Dolium "the best in environment." The winery produces approximately sixteen thousand cases of high-end wines a year, mostly malbec and cabernet sauvignon, and Laura was responsible for marketing, sales, new business, and legal matters for the winery in the United States, Europe, and Asia. Dolium has supported the local B Corp movement that culminated in September 2019 with the Mendoza +B Symposium, held locally.

Laura has volunteered for over a decade in numerous leadership positions for the global network Young Presidents' Organization (YPO), a community of twenty-nine thousand CEOs, whose membership companies add up to 10 percent of the world's GDP. She chaired the YPO Impact Network Council, the Social Engagement Network, and the Helping Disadvantaged Kids Network. She also moderated hundreds of YPO webinars that inspired and led to positive impact action. She was a major advocate within YPO on the importance of authentic triple-bottom-line corporate sustainability, and she organized webinars with many leaders in the B Corp movement and inspired many members to complete the free online B Impact Assessment by B Lab, culminating in 2020 with a joint partnership between B Lab and YPO.

For decades, she has been a public speaker on the Caring Economy, gender parity issues, impact investing, sustainability, and technology innovation solutions, and she has presented at the United Nations, YPO Leadership Summits, Prestel & Partners Forums, Kiva

U, SAP, and Opportunity Collaboration. She has presented the Non-flict methodology, the B Corp movement, and microfinance to audiences at NYU, Columbia University, Fordham University, London Business School, Franklin University Switzerland, and Lancaster University, as well as in public and private high schools. She combines her passion for engaging youth to be changemakers with her communications expertise.

As a philanthropist, educator, and social entrepreneur residing in New York City, Laura has pioneered curricula on social entrepreneurship for middle and high schools to engage the next generation of leaders in critical development issues, financial inclusion, and women's empowerment.

She serves on the advisory board of *Real Leaders* magazine, and has published articles on legal and social entrepreneurship topics for the United Nations and in the *Wall Street Journal* (*WSJ*), Huffington Post, and Argentine newspapers.

Laura is the recipient of numerous awards for her social entrepreneurship achievements, such as the United Nations Social Impact Award (2018), Real Leaders: 100 Visionary Leaders (2015), and B Corp Ambassador (2014).

LAURA AND I met at an Ellevate Network Executive Council breakfast in New York City, where we discussed her journey as an immigrant and her thoughts on leadership and making a positive impact. Laura is a formidable force for transformation and progress in our world. I am deeply moved by her commitment to live by example, tackle some of the greatest challenges of our day, and educate the next generation of leaders. She lives and breathes her values on a daily basis, by continually bringing out the positive and the best in others.

The Subversive

"*Los subversivos ya no usan armas, sino la pluma.*" ("Subversives no longer use weapons, but the pen.") Those were the words of Carlos Menem, the then President of Argentina, in response to Laura's provocative *Wall Street Journal* piece titled "Old Democratic Pitfalls Dog the New Argentina," dated March 27, 1992.

From the young Argentine attorney admitted to practice law in Argentina and in New York State in the 1980s came forth the clarion call for separation of powers in governments, especially the independence of the judiciary, and a free press in her home country. The piece condemned corruption and overreach by the executive branch. Why did Laura risk so much to publish this article? When Laura showed her parents the draft of the article—in her own name, no less, and not a pseudonym—they were scared for her and their own safety in Argentina. They pleaded with her to withdraw the publication. While she may not have written the article without some prodding from a *WSJ* reporter, after conducting research for over six months and finally completing the piece, she committed to going through with it. Although notably uncomfortable about the potential political retaliation, she determined that it was a necessary thing to do.

Upon publication in the *WSJ*, the article went viral in Argentina. It was translated into Spanish by practically every local newspaper. Yet few in Argentina knew this young, courageous attorney who lived in NYC. The next day, President Menem summoned all the media to the Casa Rosada—the national government house in Argentina. He referred to Laura as a subversive for writing the article. By Monday morning, the censorship was fully implemented. All references to the article were removed. This terrified Laura's family even more. She reflects that today, given the prevalence of social media, such a deliberate and brazen silencing of a dissenting voice by the presidency would be difficult to pull off without steady criticism and calls for accountability. Today, the situation in Argentina regarding the separation of powers is still questionable. Through a combination of social pressure and regulatory developments, anti-corruption efforts in Argentina are in flux.

Propelled by Adversity and Becoming Better

When Laura came to the United States in August 1986, her home country had recently emerged from five decades of military dictatorships. She obtained her law degree in Argentina and worked at one of the most prestigious law firms, which had few female lawyers and no female partners. This was not uncommon at the time, as most professions in Argentina were male dominated.

Dyslexia was Laura's primary challenge, and she pushed hard to overcome it. Although it had been diagnosed in Argentina, there were limited treatment options, and those who lived with dyslexia were mostly expected to adapt to the disability. As Malcolm Gladwell intimates in his book *David and Goliath: Underdogs, Misfits, and the Art of Battling Giants*, the modus operandi of most folks with dyslexia is to work very hard and continuously think and act out of the box. Gladwell shared in an interview at the Wharton School that there are so many entrepreneurs who have dyslexia. When you talk to them, they will tell you that they succeeded not in spite of their disability, but because of it. As adults, they view their disability as desirable because through their hard work, they see innovative opportunities that others may overlook. Laura is best described as resourceful because she sees problems as opportunities of growth, believes in continuous internal growth, and applies her focus to solve big and small challenges.

Laura obtained a scholarship to join the master of laws program at the University of Illinois at Urbana-Champaign. She was one of ten foreign graduates at the law school, at a time when the class consisted of two hundred graduates. In spite of this, she was committed to obtaining a legal job and remaining in the United States. She needed an employer who was willing to file for permanent residency for her. She aggressively sent out letters to law firms until she landed a job with a prestigious Wall Street law firm. Laura appreciates that in the United States, hard work pays off. If you work hard, you see tangible results in your career. Her motto was "In the USA, there are opportunities at every corner"; regardless of your origin, you just have to listen, observe, and work hard! In Argentina, these opportunities were not commonplace. Most of the time, one needed to know someone in order to move up.

Laura chose law because in Argentina, the prevailing view was that for a woman to succeed professionally, she had to study one of the "hard" professions: law, medicine, engineering, or economics.

Laura came to the United States in 1986 alone, with a full scholarship from the University of Illinois. The principal challenges she navigated were loneliness and learning the English language while being dyslexic. These pushed her to work harder all the time.

While she was in Argentina, she was constantly around family and friends. Her parents immigrated to Argentina from Italy in the 1960s, and for them, family time was important—eating together was highly valued. Laura had never experienced the loneliness she felt while working the very long hours required at the Wall Street law firm, and she became intimately familiar with the feeling of loneliness and total self-sufficiency. Her family visited sporadically, and that helped to occasionally ease the pain.

A Catalyst for Social Impact and Change

Along with her brother, Laura now manages the family wine business in Mendoza, Argentina. Laura believes that wine making is an art, and she is very proud of transforming the business into the first environmentally sustainable winery in Latin America; it was granted a B Corp certification in early 2014 and was awarded the "Best of the Environment" by B Lab.

Certified B Corporations are a new kind of business that balance purpose and profit. Today, they are required to consider the impact of their decisions on their "stakeholders": workers, customers, suppliers, community, and the environment. The B Corp movement is a community of business leaders, driving a global movement of people using business as a force for good.

Inspiring the Next Generation

Laura is also passionate about inspiring the next generation of leaders. She has promoted microfinance (one of the most successful types of social entrepreneurship) to be learned early, both by enabling high school students to found microfinance clubs in their institutions and by supporting the industry in many ways.

Laura coproduced and cocreated the educational material for the *Who Cares?* documentary, which has been adopted into a high school curriculum to promote social entrepreneurship among high school students.

Laura is also passionate about the importance of the skill of empathy in our society, as she believes the world needs more emotional intelligence at every level. This can start as early as three years old in prekindergarten with the curriculum of Think Equal, an NGO that provides globally one of the most effective and affordable methodologies for social emotional learning. In partnership with Ashoka, Laura has supported and helped scale in many ways the Start Empathy program, including by getting the Teach For All program to use it. She believes the world desperately needs emotional intelligence in order to overcome our two most burning issues: inequality and climate crisis.

Daily Rituals and Words to Live By

One of Laura's daily practices is to be authentically grateful as a morning and evening ritual. Every day before getting out of bed, she asks herself, *What I am grateful for?* She writes every day in her Five-Minute Journal the three things she's grateful for and the three things that will make her day special.

Laura firmly believes that readers are leaders, and books have been one of the joys in her life. She immerses herself in learning by reading inspiring authors. Reading is an incredibly gratifying and effective way to learn in just a few hours the essence of what took others a lifelong journey to learn.

Laura also practices active listening to others with an open heart, mind, ears, and eyes. The key to being a good communicator is listening to others. The secret is to put yourself in the shoes of the person you're listening to. In addition to empathy, curiosity is key. It's important to authentically engage by asking yourself questions and asking questions to others. This is the best way to learn and adapt to new culture. Relatedly, this is the best way to become a good communicator.

Laura's Definition of Success

Laura believes success is a personal journey, where one finds personal fulfillment, as well as professional and financial success. In essence, success is finding life-work harmony, no matter how complex and challenging the circumstances are. Making money is definitely not enough to find success; an attitude of continuous learning and finding a strong bond with others are key to finding fulfillment.

Laura learned this the hard way. In the 1980s and '90s, success as a lawyer meant working eighty hours a week and bringing in clients. Balancing this with success as a mother was quite challenging. One of Laura's big aha moments regarding gender inequality was when she tried to keep up her career while juggling the care of the kids, household, and a husband. Her stress level was so high that cancer knocked on her door and forced her to reassess and reevaluate what mattered most at that moment. Her priorities shifted, and what mattered to her the most was not her career, but seeing her kids become independent, courageous, and good global citizens. But, in making this choice, she was seen as giving up a "successful" career on Wall Street.

Success today is about continued personal growth—transforming oneself, leading by example, inspiring, supporting, and motivating the transformation of others. Laura is motivated by working from the inside out and using what is around her to inspire and transform others to a more Caring Economy. Leadership is not simply about creating awareness and inspiring with one's own behaviors; it is about inspiring people, so that each individual can become the best version of themselves and perform at their highest potential, given that every human being is wonderful and has unique and special qualities.

True leadership, as embodied by Gandhi, Florence Nightingale, Virginia Woolf, Frida Kahlo, Ruth Bader Ginsburg, Marie Curie, the Mirabal sisters, Malala Yousafzai, Gertrude Bell, Barbara Strozzi, Alessandra Giliani, and Gaitana is also demonstrated by the innumerable anonymous women that have struggled, that have supported women's values of caring and respect for others, and that have led the way so that today, women can study from an early age, have a profession, vote, own property, decide to marry for love, lead countries, run businesses, and have the freedom that women of decision possessed ten thousand years ago in prehistoric times, before patriarchal values dominated.

LAURA'S IMMIGRACE

- Gender parity changemaker
- Peacemaker: conflict-resolutions advocate and coach
- System social entrepreneur
- Impact investor
- Innovative educator
- Philanthropist

LAURA'S IMMIGEMS

◇ *Recognize the opportunities in every corner.* During the course of over thirty years in the United States, Laura has seen that there are opportunities for personal and professional growth in every corner. One only has to "walk to the corner," and magic happens. No matter what life brings, there is a gift in it. We only need to be willing to seek it out and work hard to master the skills required to see those opportunities come to full fruition. The fruits of those opportunities belong to the disciplined, focused, and hardworking. With clarity of purpose and integrity, you will find personal, professional, and financial fulfillment. Work hard, not only at a job, but on internal growth and learning.

◇ *View conflict as an opportunity to grow.* Rather than viewing conflict as something to be feared or avoided, the Nonflict Way offers a simple, effective three-step method to face conflicts (which, in essence, are not good or bad) and transform them into opportunities to grow in patience, empathy, and in our understanding of others. The three steps include: understanding one's self and the other; understanding your shared reality; and cocreating the future.

◇ *Identify a mentor.* Mentorship is key. Be inquisitive. Research your mentors' careers, and connect with them emotionally and intellectually.

16.
Blend Differences and Create Strength

ADELA WILLIAMS
Talent-Acquisition Strategist

dela Roxana Williams relocated to New Jersey at age four from Peru in 1981. She studied psychology and business management at Essex County College and University of Phoenix. Following graduation, due to her passion for helping individuals establish long-term career goals, she worked in human resources in a recruiting role. With support from her family and friends, Adela began working as an independent recruiter helping to connect organizations with high-quality talent.

Adela is a talent-acquisition and brand awareness specialist at Family First Funding LLC. She was previously a talent-acquisition specialist at VMC Group, a world leader in the design and manufacture of vibration isolation, seismic control, and shock-protection products.

In her free time, Adela enjoys music, physical fitness, outdoor activities, and spending time with her three children.

ONE OF MY favorite things about living in Sparta, New Jersey, is the amazing moms who are part of my circle of friends. My friendship with the mom squad began when I met Adela a number of years ago at a spaghetti dinner at our kids' school. She, in turn, introduced me to the most fabulous group of moms in town. From paint night to dinner and dancing, boat rides to Olympic-themed beach parties, these incredible women have shown me what friendship and sisterhood is, and they are pure love.

No, You Can't Take Her Home with You

It was the middle of the night when eleven-year-old Adela smelled smoke and heard chaos outside her window. Unsure whether it was a dream, nightmare, or hallucination, she stumbled across the dark hallway to her parents' bedroom. There was a massive fire, and her dad only had his underwear on as the family rushed out of the house in a panic.

Adela's grandma's home burned to the ground, and the fire left the family with nothing. Her grandma was in a bitter property battle at the time, so they suspected arson. The family was grateful to be alive and safe.

One of the firefighters who had helped ensure her family's safety asked whether he could take Adela home to his wife—as if Adela were a pet! He wanted to help; his wife wanted a child, and they could take care of her, he said. In that moment, Adela realized that she was viewed differently from the "normal" American. Think how unlikely it would be for such a request to be directed at a white American parent. And think how any parent, regardless of their race, would feel under those circumstances. Adela's mother held her tightly, looked the firefighter in the eye, and firmly responded, "No."

More Beautiful than Real Estate

Adela was born in Lima, Peru. Her father was American, born in Italy, and his family invested in real estate around the world and had gone to Peru on business. There, he found something more beautiful—love.

After her father returned to the United States, Adela's mom discovered that she was pregnant with Adela. It was not until four years later that her father returned to Peru. Her parents reunited, and Adela and her mom relocated to the United States, where her parents were married.

People often struggle to place a finger on Adela's background, based on her physical appearance alone. In response to the frequently asked question "Where are you from?," Adela used to say, "The United States." Lately, however, she asks whether they want to know about her nationality, and she proceeds to provide details. She's learned that people have more of an appreciation and interest in the international aspects of her culture. She also emphasizes that she is, quite simply, "the result of love."

Newark's Great Melting Pot

Spanish was Adela's first language, but because she came to the United States at such a young age, she quickly picked up English. Her dad only spoke to her in English. Her mom would speak to the kids (Adela and her younger brother and sister, who eventually came along) in Spanish, but they were only allowed to respond in English.

Adela also learned Italian. The young family lived with Adela's grandmother—her dad's mom—who had a large home in Newark, New Jersey.

Adela attended E. Alma Flagg School in Newark. Young Adela perceived it a bit like a prison. The entire school had only two windows, and the children were required to line up for everything!

Newark was, of course, a massive melting pot in the early 1980s. Adela's friends were diverse, and she interacted with people from different cultures and backgrounds—Italians, African Americans, white Americans, and almost every conceivable nationality and ethnic group. This blending of cultures taught her to embrace all cultures. As she got older, she noticed division around her and that people often judged others based on their culture, ethnic group, and economic status.

Adela had a sense of being a melting pot herself—Peruvian, Italian, and American culture were all key ingredients that formed her.

Adela's mom's adjustment to the United States was more difficult for two reasons. She was adjusting to a new country and customs but also to her husband's Italian family. Adela's mom had no friends or family in the United States. She had left family and friends in Peru and had embraced her husband's Italian family and identity. In some ways, it felt like some of Adela's mom's own identity was lost. Her mom evolved from making traditional Peruvian dishes, such as ceviche, to mostly Italian recipes, such as pasta. Her mom's clothing choices also changed.

Adela's mother found her sound sense of identity by throwing herself into work. She had been a seamstress in Peru. In the United States, she continued down this path by making dog beds and coats. She visited Peru often, and whenever she did, Adela missed having her around. Adela also found herself being a six-year-old mom to her sister whenever her mom was away. Adela couldn't imagine her own daughter stepping into such a role when she was six years old.

A Blending of Passions

As with most things in her life, Adela's career path is a blending. She blends real estate work with being a recruiter. She enjoys helping people with things that matter to them. Nothing is more central to our lives than our career paths and the homes we live in.

Adela naturally enjoys watching people succeed and appreciates people who strive to enjoy their passions in life. She started out by working as an administrative assistant for executives at a telecom company and was acknowledged for coaching people through their job roles. One of her managers suggested that she try the human resources administrative function to help assist with the onboarding of new employees. She was successful and quickly began to help hiring managers find the best resources to fill roles.

As a recruiter, Adela enjoys selling people's skills and putting their most important skills forward. She became a recruiter when a former boss first saw this unique skill in her, noting that she saw things that others didn't. Beyond identifying candidates to fill specific roles, she has the ability to draw out skills in people and sell those skills to companies and organizations that need them. It is ironic that she has this unique ability to see talent in others, but it took someone else to see talent in her and to encourage her to bring that forth and make it part of her life's work. How often this happens to us—it takes others recognizing our potential to call us to step more fully into living it.

Workplace Diversity

Adela is passionate about diversity in the workplace. To Adela, diversity is about knowledge and strength. She values intellectual diversity borne of different cultural experiences. She appreciates differences in talent, educational background, mindset, experiences, cultures, and customs—all blended together to form strengths and superior enhancements of the mind and life.

When she worked for a large telecom company, she once implemented a pilot program where she encouraged the team of recruiters to look at all the résumés that included candidates' names. Not surprisingly, they selected mostly white males, some Asians, and lots of Ivy League graduates.

They were then urged to review a different pile of résumés, without names and schools. In this instance, they selected and hired top-performing diverse talent. The company adopted this approach as a way to eliminate unconscious bias that could come into play in the recruiting process and hinder a company's ability to select high-performing talent.

In a TED Talk titled "Why the Best Hire May Not Have the Perfect Résumé," Regina Hartley describes two types of candidates: the "silver spoon" candidate (one who clearly had advantages and was destined for success) and the "scrapper" (a candidate who had to fight against tremendous odds to get to the same point). Hartley shares her own powerful scrapper story. She grew up in a family with a father who was diagnosed with paranoid schizophrenia and couldn't hold a job, in spite of his brilliance: "Our lives were one part *Cuckoo's Nest*, one part *Awakenings*, and one part *A Beautiful Mind*." She urges companies to give the "scrapper" a chance: "Choose the underestimated contender, whose secret weapons are passion and purpose. Hire the scrapper."

Adela believes that candidates who blend Ivy League degrees with scrapper attributes can be golden hires.

Speaking multiple languages has been a tremendous advantage in Adela's work. It enables her to relate to job seekers who are immigrants or children of immigrants. Many immigrants in the workforce feel more confident joining forces with companies who appreciate cultural diversity. Those candidates are able to utilize their skills and backgrounds to advance the companies' missions and values in the world.

Adela's Definition of Success

Adela defines success as happiness and strength: being happy enhances our strengths. Happiness is that positive energy that focuses on solutions. Happy people are positive and appreciative. Regardless of what you have around you physically, you will not be successful if you do not have a positive outlook and appreciation for life.

ADELA'S IMMIGRACE

- Talent and diversity strategist blending passion and purpose for the fulfillment of human potential and the advancement of organizational missions.

ADELA'S IMMIGEMS

◊ *Listen.* It is important to understand what is being said and to not substitute what others are saying for your own beliefs. Adela sees this on teams—both when she coaches her kids' sports teams and interacts with various businesses for recruiting. People often substitute what is being communicated to them with what they want to hear.

◊ *Surround yourself with people who are smarter than you.* Surround yourself with people that are like great books—rich in knowledge and experiences and generous in sharing those. This enables you to continually grow.

◊ *Act decisively.* Make it your business to quickly understand the lay of the land, and then make a decision. Assess your options and possible consequences of the decision.

17.
Rise Above

| **UGO UKABAM**
| Trailblazing Labor and Employment Attorney

U go Ukabam is senior counsel of labor and employment law at General Mills. In this position, she has employment law oversight for all General Mills international locations, some of the corporate function, as well as the Innovation, Technology, and Quality Organization. Prior to joining General Mills in 2011, Ugo was a partner at the Minnesota law firm of Gray Plant Mooty, and she was the first racial-minority female to achieve that status in the firm's over-140-year history at the time. Ugo has also served as an adjunct professor of law at Mitchell Hamline School of Law in Saint Paul. Before relocating to the United States, Ugo worked for Mobil Producing Nigeria, Unlimited (now ExxonMobil), and Diamond Bank Plc., in Lagos, Nigeria. She has an LLM from Harvard Law School, a JD from Mitchell Hamline School of Law, and an LLB from the University of Nigeria.

Ugo's awards and recognitions include being one of *Minnesota Lawyer* magazine's Inaugural In-House Counsel Honorees in 2019; recognized as a Rising Star by *Minnesota Law & Politics* in 2009 and 2010; and receiving the Lena O. Smith Achievement Award from the Minnesota Black Women Lawyers Network in 2009. The award is given to an individual who exemplifies the spirit of courage and leadership, epitomizes the highest goals and traditions of the profession, and advances opportunities for women within the legal profession. In 2015, Ugo was named a fellow of the Leadership Council on Legal Diversity. She is one of a small number of high-potential attorneys nationwide selected for this national leadership development program designed to increase diversity in the legal profession.

Ugo is active in the Hennepin County Bar Association in various leadership roles—current member and past cochair of the Diversity Committee; member of the Nominating Committee; and past cochair of the Employment Law section. She serves as a mentor to other lawyers, law students, and aspiring law students. Ugo also sits on the Mitchell Hamline School of Law Board of Trustees and most currently served on the Dean Search Committee that recruited the current dean and president of the school. Ugo is very active in her Nigerian community and currently serves on the board of the Igbo Women League of Minnesota.

In her spare time, Ugo loves to travel around the world, and she has visited over thirty countries so far. She is blessed with two sons, Majeed and Sam. She also has three parakeets: Henrietta, Cleo, and Summer.

I FIRST MET Ugo at the Association of Black Lawyers gala in Minnesota in 2010. Her reputation preceded her, as the first racial-minority female to make partner at her Minneapolis law firm. She is tall, graceful, and immensely poised. She leads by example and inspires others through her commitment to excellence, service, and advocacy.

A Catalyst for Change

Ugo and her friends sat in the downtown Minneapolis restaurant, waiting to be served. Tables that were seated after them had already been served. Ugo had observed that whenever she went to this restaurant with friends of color, they waited an unusually long time to be served. This never happened when she went to the restaurant with Caucasian colleagues.

At first, she didn't share this observation with anyone because she hadn't ruled out the possibility that it was pure coincidence.

On this day, however, she mentioned it to her friends, who noted that they had observed the same practice at the restaurant. They, too, had looked for other possible explanations when it happened. Perhaps it was an especially busy time of the day. Perhaps the restaurant was short-staffed. Perhaps their section was being served by a slower waiter. Perhaps . . .

Ugo couldn't shake the feeling that it wasn't a coincidence, so she brought it to a manager's attention. The manager took the complaint seriously, expressed gratitude that she raised it, and committed to look into it.

Subsequently, the owner of the restaurant met with Ugo at the law office where she worked at the time. He apologized profusely for his employees' conduct and made a commitment that such conduct would have no place at the restaurant going forward. Ugo genuinely loves this restaurant and still goes there to this day. She is grateful that she spoke up, and she subsequently noticed a remarkable change in customer service. The truth is that when employees develop poor practices in one area, they likely adopt them in others as well. In the end, the positive shift improved the overall service at the restaurant.

The cogent lesson from Ugo's experience with the restaurant is to speak up and take action against racism and other forms of injustice when we encounter them. No one can guarantee specific outcomes, but when we make excuses, minimize, or justify these practices, we further entrench them and contribute to injustice in our world.

Seeds of Service

Born in Nigeria during the height of the civil war, Ugo's family fled Port Harcourt for their hometown of Arondizuogu. She is one of nine children (eight surviving). Her father was a headmaster turned entrepreneur, and her mother was a businesswoman. The seeds of her love for service were sewn at this early stage in her life. Ugo was deeply inspired by her parents' example, and she learned valuable life and leadership lessons from the way they served their community. Many in the community looked to her parents as pillars of strength, wisdom, and counsel.

In a 2017 interview with *Hennepin Lawyer*, Ugo shared, "My family is made up of outspoken people with a passion for service, so I was trained from a young age to speak up for people and use my moral compass." She continued, "I believe in respect for the human person and the rights which flow from human dignity." Ugo is a devout Catholic and credits her faith for her passion for social justice.

After she obtained a law degree from the University of Nigeria, Ugo worked for ExxonMobil Nigeria (then called Mobil Producing Nigeria) in Lagos for two years. She subsequently worked in the personnel department at Diamond Bank. Ugo left Diamond Bank for Harvard Law School, where she obtained an LLM with a focus on business law.

Following the completion of her LLM, Ugo lived in Doha, Qatar, for two years before returning to Nigeria. After a few months in Nigeria, she returned to the United States.

A one-year degree for foreign-trained attorneys, the LLM is not designed to prepare foreign attorneys for US legal practice. It is designed for lawyers who wish to return to their home countries with foundational knowledge of US law. Most foreign attorneys who obtain LLMs and decide to enter the US workforce often find it difficult to do so. When Ugo decided to practice law in the United States, she knew it would be best to obtain a Juris Doctor degree, and this was when she enrolled in Mitchell Hamline School of Law, then William Mitchell College of Law.

Ugo's Leadership Crucible

Ugo was not your average law student. Most law students are twenty-something years old, attend law school right out of college, and generally have few commitments outside of law school. Law school is challenging enough for the single student without parental responsibilities. Ugo was a single mother with two toddlers and was going through a difficult divorce. Somewhere between mastering legal theories and keeping the kids warm during the merciless Minnesota winters lay Ugo's leadership crucible. The challenges of those years of law school formed her in ways she'd never anticipated.

The first set of challenges was financial. Paying for school was itself a big adjustment, as her family had covered her educational expenses in Nigeria. In addition, her childcare expenses were higher than her law school tuition. Ugo worked, cared for her children, and studied like her life depended on it.

The law school years taught Ugo valuable lessons in prioritization, as she had little wiggle room in her schedule. Another valuable lesson was that the best support systems are not necessarily purchased with money. Family, friends, and supportive law school professors and staff jumped in to help Ugo to be her best at school and take care of her children. When childcare plans fell through, she would drop the children off at the Multicultural Affairs office at the law school while she attended class. Ugo's Family Law professor also provided excellent counsel as she went through the challenging divorce. Her sister visited from the UK to babysit during her law school final examinations. In spite of all these extraordinary circumstances, Ugo graduated from law school magna cum laude.

The stress and tension of legal study is magnified during preparation for the bar examination. For this challenge, Ugo's sister took her two sons to the UK for the entire summer!

Ugo believes she would never have made it through those years without the support of her family, friends, and generous law school staff. For them, she's immensely grateful. Along with her family upbringing in Nigeria, these people inspire her to serve her community and to help others who need to be pulled up.

Advocate for Equal Opportunity

Ugo began her legal career as a summer associate at Gray Plant Mooty, one of Minneapolis's premier law firms. She began as a litigation associate and subsequently joined the employment law group. She made partner in five years. Ugo has represented employers in both federal and state courts around the country; administrative actions before the Equal Employment Opportunity Commission and the Minnesota Department of Human Rights; and other state and federal agencies.

After eight and a half years at Gray Plant Mooty, she joined General Mills as labor and employment law counsel. Part of the reason Ugo chose to work for General Mills is that the companies' values are aligned with hers. She thrives in their culture of nourishing lives—making them healthier, easier, and richer—and giving back to community.

Ugo believes that social justice and corporate law are not mutually exclusive. She uses her in-house role to influence policies and training and to ensure that people are being treated fairly and equally.

Ugo's Definition of Success

A firm believer in balanced success, one of the principles Ugo lives by is from Zig Ziglar: "The foundation stones for a balanced success are honesty, character, integrity, faith, love, and loyalty."

She also believes that we make a living by what we give. She is passionate about giving back—to her family, as a devoted mother to her boys (now young men), and to her community, through mentoring, service, and advocacy.

UGO'S IMMIGRACE

- Trailblazing attorney
- Advocate and change agent

UGO'S IMMIGEMS

◇ *Work hard and build relationships.* There is no substitute for hard work and for building strong relationships.

◇ *Be a person of unquestionable integrity.* In order for people to entrust significant things to you, they must trust you.

◇ *Have faith.* Through all the challenges she has encountered, Ugo's faith in God has remained unshaken and has guided her through it all.

Immigrace Journal

1. How will I voluntarily embrace discomfort every day in order to grow?

   _____

   _____

   _____

2. In what three principal ways can I innovate in my industry, business, or professional life?

   _____

   _____

   _____

3. In what area of my life have I become complacent, and in what area do I need to innovate?

   _____

   _____

   _____

4. What in my life today must change?

   _____

   _____

   _____

5. If leaders anticipate and losers react, in what areas of life and work do I need to be more proactive?

_____

_____

_____

6. What daily ritual will I integrate into my life to spark creativity and innovation?

_____

_____

_____

7. What weekly ritual will I integrate into my life to spark creativity and innovation?

_____

_____

_____

8. What makes me feel playful?

_____

_____

_____

9. How will I integrate play into my work?

_____

_____

_____

10. How will I integrate play into my personal life?

_____

_____

_____

11. What will I do at least once a year to support my ongoing personal development? (This could be a retreat, conference, seminar, or similar event.)

_____

_____

_____

Chinwe's Definition of Success

Success is joy and living my potential. It is realizing, honing, growing, and sharing my gifts with the world, while being joyful, healthy, and radiant. It is living and experiencing the best in the world, while embodying and reflecting something transcendent, infinitely loving, and divine.

Og Mandino, author of *The Greatest Salesman in the World*, once said: "I am here for a purpose and that purpose is to grow into a mountain, not to shrink to a grain of sand. . . . I will strain my potential until it cries for mercy."

The idea of my potential crying for mercy always brings a smile to my face because I've lived it. Yet, if I improve the world around me and well beyond it, to the far reaches of the earth, while being joyful and bringing joy to those I love, that, to me, is success.

Conclusion
To Your Brilliant Journey!

Thank you for journeying with me across all the continents of the world and across the United States to gather the rarest of gems and to redefine the face of genius.

I hope you not only enjoyed the journeys and stories, but that you will accept the invitation to write and rewrite your own story. I hope you revisit this book as a resource for inspiration, that you use the Brilliance Blueprint as a guide and the Immigrace Journal as your companion on your very own remarkable journey, and that you live the life you were born to live!

For more immigrace inspiration, tune in to the Brilliance Beyond Borders podcast, which has featured conversations with: Naz Barouti (Iran-born lawyer, author, entrepreneur, media commentator, and public speaker); Orlena Nwokah Blanchard (Canada-born marketing executive multi-cultural marketing expert, who spent her formative years in Nigeria and the United States, and is a bi-lingual citizen of four countries); Dr. Adebola Dele-Michael (US-born board certified dermatologist, entrepreneur, and trailblazing beauty expert, who spent her formative years in Nigeria); Ekene Onu (US-born executive coach and feminine leadership expert, who spent her formative years in Nigeria); Luciane Serifovic (Brazil-born luxury real estate powerhouse, thought leader, and CEO); and Uni Yost (South Korea-born, serial entrepreneur, business and technology visionary, and relationship builder).

Also visit chinweesimai.com, where we explore a range of topics of interest to professional women, including executive presence, self-awareness, habits, mentoring, and transforming the pressure to excel.

$$/ˌmanəˈfestō/$$
a written statement declaring publicly the intentions,
motives, or views of its issuer

The word has its origins in the mid-seventeenth century: from Italian—manifestare; from Latin—manifestus (obvious); also from Latin—manifesto (make public); and from English—manifest.

Every freedom movement needs a manifesto—a public declaration of its motives and intentions. This immigrace movement to democratize genius is no different. Although we are not a political movement in the traditional sense, our quest is every bit about human freedom. There've been movements in history that have used manifestoes to suppress the dignity of human beings. Some of those abusers have been discussed in this book. But they don't have the final word. We must continually reclaim the term as a tool for human freedom and as a vehicle for truth. The manifesto makes obvious your intentions, and serves as a powerful reminder of who you are, regardless of the circumstances around you.

IMMIGRACE MANIFESTO

I am remarkable.
I say yes to my immigrace and discover my genius.
I commit to inner self-mastery and joy.
I dare to play in the big leagues.
I set and accomplish big intentions and goals.
I transform failure.
I embrace change and innovate.
I serve those around me.
I renew the world.
I am brilliance beyond borders.

Acknowledgments

Immense appreciation to the women featured in these pages. Thank you for your vulnerability and generosity, and for sharing your stories and immigems so that others may embrace the beauty of their immigrace.

To my soul sisters—Chioma Eze, Vivian Guzman, Ndidi Obidoa, Chinwe Osondu, Aku Aghazu, Ify Oyeka, Nkem Igwebuike, Nkem Oguchi, Tracy Ileka, Ogo Ekaidem, Chioma Osondu, Michelle Sorro, Cassandra Jean-Baptiste, Indira Bernhard, Tyesha Miley, Maggie Awad, Mary Presberg, and the Sparta Mom Squad: I love you, ladies!

To the wise Professor George McKenna, the first person in the United States to see a glimmer of potential in me: you inspire me to extend your brilliant legacy by recognizing potential in others.

To Brian Hepp, Brian Nunez, David Lawrence, and Crystal and Ray McGuire: you are forces of greatness! You challenge me, make me a better leader, and are examples of the highest human potential and integrity. I'm enormously grateful.

To Team Legacy: I couldn't ask for a more legendary group to ignite me on the mission of the advancement of our people.

To Team Harper Horizon—Andrea Fleck-Nisbet, Amanda Bauch, and John Andrade: you are the most exceptional publishing family any author could dream of.

To my literary agent, Leticia Gomez of Savvy Literary, as well as the entire Ascendant Global family (Nicole Anderson, Merilee Kern, Seun Ariyo, Raoul Davis, and Kathy Palokoff), my editor, Candace Johnson, and my book coach, Lisa Tener: I'm enormously thankful for your commitment and dedicated service.

To my extraordinary intern, Mackenzie Rutherford; Destiny Davis; and Ni-Ka Ford: thank you for being such gems.

To my dearest family (uncles, aunts, cousins, and in-laws) and friends; mentees; Federal Government Girls' College, Owerri Class of 1994; colleagues (past and present, especially Goldman Sachs alumni; Citi Anti-Bribery team; Turner Herbert; Harold Butler and Citi Black Managing Directors): oceans of gratitude for you.

To the Padres, especially Bob Connor, Kamil Kiszka, David McDonnell, Michael Okere, Kenny Udumka, and John Higgins: thank you for grounding me in my truest anchor forever.

Appendix A
Immigrace Journal Exercises

Say Yes to Your Immigrace: *Discover Your Genius*

1. Who do I want to be in the world?

2. What dreams have been entrusted to me? What are some things I believe in my gut that I'm meant to do in this world? (It could be one thing, or it could be ten.)

3. What are three things I enjoyed doing as a child?

4. What are three activities that make me feel creative?

5. What activities do I get lost in? What can I do for hours without realizing the passage of time? These don't have to be careers or professional activities.

    _____

    _____

    _____

6. If no one (including me) could talk me out of it, what three possible careers paths would I follow?

    _____

    _____

7. In what areas of my life am I living my genius?

    a. Three activities that represent living my genius professionally:

        _____

        _____

        _____

    b. Three activities that represent living my genius personally:

        _____

        _____

        _____

8. What new, higher expression of me is waiting to be brought to life?

    _____

    _____

    _____

9. I commit to doing these three things to develop my genius over the next three months:

    _____

    _____

    _____

10. Who can support me in nurturing my genius? (Think mentor, coach, or teacher.)

11. My purpose in this world is:

12. The grandest vision of my life includes:

BRILLIANCE BLUEPRINT #2
Inner Self-Mastery: *Find Joy*

1. What are the top three negative experiences of my life?

2. What did I learn from those experiences?

3. Why can I be grateful for them?

4. How will I continue to support myself to grow through them?

5. Who has the expertise to support me to grow through them? (Choose wisely. Various circumstances will require different sorts of expertise. For example, grief, depression, marriage/family, and business challenges call for radically different skill sets. Choose experts who have attained the results you seek, either for themselves or for other clients. Resist the temptation to conflate success, e.g., taking marriage advice from a celebrity who may have attained success as a movie star, but who hasn't attained the results you'd like to see in your own marriage.)

———————————————————————————

———————————————————————————

———————————————————————————

6. How will I nourish my faith and spiritual life?

    a. Daily ———————————————————————

    b. Weekly ——————————————————————

    c. Monthly ——————————————————————

    d. Yearly ——————————————————————

7. How will I find my joy every day?

———————————————————————————

———————————————————————————

———————————————————————————

8. Three things that make me happy:

———————————————————————————

———————————————————————————

———————————————————————————

9. True happiness is:

———————————————————————————

———————————————————————————

———————————————————————————

10. True fulfillment is:

_____

_____

_____

11. I'm happy when:

_____

_____

_____

12. I'll contribute to my happiness every day by:

_____

_____

_____

13. Emotion is energy in motion. We can gain mastery of our emotions by recognizing and acknowledging them and by understanding them as things we do and engage in (as opposed to things that happen to us).

    a. Three positive emotions I regularly engage in are:

       _____

       _____

       _____

    b. Three negative emotions I regularly engage in are:

       _____

       _____

       _____

14. I'll manage my emotions by:

_____

_____

_____

15. What are my values?

_____

_____

_____

(I'm astounded by how few adults actually know what they value and do not. Part of owning your journey is owning your place in the world and the things that drive you. It's been said that individuals are often motivated by increasing pleasure and avoiding pain. Values are emotional states that we believe are important to experience or avoid.

Our values can change over time, but lack of awareness is a true immigrace killer. If you don't know what you value, you are guaranteeing that you will not live your purpose in life, that you will likely be unhappy, and that you'll advance others' values.

Examples of values we move toward: joy, freedom, peace, adventure, success, love, trust, courage, empathy, growth, faith, passion, security, achievement, compassion.

Examples of values we avoid: sadness, sorrow, failure, rejection, anger, loneliness, depression, boredom, apathy, guilt, helplessness, frustration.)

BRILLIANCE BLUEPRINT #3
Dare to Play in the Big Leagues: *Set and Accomplish Big Goals*

Ready, Set, Goals!

1. What are my goals for this quarter?

    a. Faith/Spirituality/Contribution

    _____

    _____

    _____

    b. Finances

    _____

    _____

    _____

    c. Work/Career/Mission

    _____

    _____

    _____

d. Managing Time

_____

_____

_____

e. Relationships

_____

_____

_____

f. Managing Emotions/Meaning

_____

_____

_____

g. Health/Wellness/Physical Body

_____

_____

_____

2. Fighting for My Legacy

a. Define it. What do I want my life to stand for?

_____

_____

_____

b. How can I live my legacy? Not just leave a legacy when I'm gone, but how can I live a life of legacy?

_____

_____

_____

c. How do I wish to write my life story and what are my most important outcomes?

_____

_____

_____

d. How do I choose to focus—my time, my resources, and my talents?

_____

_____

_____

e. What must I eliminate?

_____

_____

_____

f. What can I do that will tap into my unique background and interests?

_____

_____

_____

g. Is it time for a radical change, and how can I begin to invest in a new direction?

_____

_____

_____

h. Who must I become in order to live a meaningful and impactful life?

_____

_____

_____

3. Habits Audit

a. What are the top three great habits I would love to keep:

_____

_____

_____

b. What are the top three bad habits I would love to change:

_____

_____

_____

BRILLIANCE BLUEPRINT #4
Transform Failure

1. What are three major life experiences I've defined as failures?

    _____

    _____

    _____

2. What lessons did I take from those experiences?

    _____

    _____

    _____

3. What role have they played in my journey?

    _____

    _____

    _____

4. How can I grow through them?

    _____

    _____

    _____

5. How can I use my "why" to reframe those experiences?

    _____

    _____

    _____

BRILLIANCE BLUEPRINT #5
Embrace Change and Innovate

1. How will I voluntarily embrace discomfort every day in order to grow?

    _____

    _____

    _____

2. In what three principal ways can I innovate in my industry, business, or professional life?

_____

_____

_____

3. In what area of my life have I become complacent, and in what area do I need to innovate?

_____

_____

_____

4. What in my life today must change?

_____

_____

_____

5. If leaders anticipate and losers react, in what areas of life and work do I need to be more proactive?

_____

_____

_____

6. What daily ritual will I integrate into my life to spark creativity and innovation?

_____

_____

_____

7. What weekly ritual will I integrate into my life to spark creativity and innovation?

_____

_____

_____

8. How will I integrate play into my work?

_____

_____

_____

9. How will I integrate play into my personal life?

   _____

   _____

   _____

10. What will I do at least once a year to support my ongoing personal development? (This could be a retreat, conference, seminar, or similar event.)

    _____

    _____

    _____

Appendix B
Resource Guide

CHAPTER 2

The Chinese Cultural Revolution as History (Studies of the Walter H. Shorenstein Asia-Pacific Research Center) by Joseph W. Esherick, Paul G. Pickowicz and Andrew G. Walder (Editors)

Fractured Rebellion: The Beijing Red Guard Movement by Andrew G. Walder

Blood Red Sunset: A Memoir of the Chinese Cultural Revolution by Ma Bo

Proletarian Power: Shanghai in the Cultural Revolution (Transitions—Asia and Asian America) by Elizabeth Perry and Li Xun

CHAPTER 4

Bolinao 52 (a 2008 documentary about Vietnamese boat people)

Stateless (a 2013 documentary about long-stayer Vietnamese asylum seekers in the Philippines)

From Chaos to Karuna by Mai-Phương Nguyễn (a memoir in progress about the Vietnam War and a child refugee turned medicine woman and healer, told through herstories)

CHAPTER 6

First They Killed My Father (a 2017 Netflix documentary)

Out of the Dark: Into the Garden of Hope by Dr. Sam Keo (self-published, Bloomington, IN: iUniverse, Inc., 2011)

CHAPTER 9

The Brookings Institution compiled several key resources on the Iranian Revolution in this blog post: "Order from Chaos: What to read to understand the 1979 Iranian revolution" by Suzanne Maloney, Eliora Katz, and Keian Razipour, https://www.brookings.edu/blog/order-from-chaos/2019/01/28/what-to-read-to-understand-the-1979-iranian-revolution/

CHAPTER 10

People Power, an Eyewitness History: The Philippine Revolution of 1986 by Monina A. Mercado

CHAPTER 14

Refusenik (a 2007 documentary; more information about it here: www.refusenikmovie.com)

The Refusenik Project (a free educational resource: https://www.refusenikproject.org/history/)

CHAPTER 17

The Insider: Stories of War and Peace From Nigeria by Achebe, Chinua; Ifejika, Samuel, Nwankwo, Artur; Nwapa, Flora (Contributors), https://www.abaa.org/book/736803446

The Nigerian Revolution and the Biafran War by Alexander A. Madiebo

There Was a Country: A Personal History of Biafra by Chinua Achebe

The Biafra Story: The Making of an African Legend by Frederick Forsyth

The Politics of Biafra: And the Future of Nigeria by Chudi Ofodile

Notes

INTRODUCTION

1. "Employment Status of the Foreign-born and Native-born Populations by Selected Characteristics, 2019-2020 Annual Averages," Bureau of Labor statistics, updated May 18, 2021, https://www.bls.gov/news.release/forbrn.t01.htm.
2. *Wall Street Journal*, "Women in the Workplace 2020," accessed May 13, 2021, https://www.wsj.com/news/collection/women-in-the-workplace-2020-691c54f4.

HOW THIS BOOK IS STRUCTURED

1. "Construction of the Taj Mahal," Landmarks of the World, https://www.wonders-of-the-world.net/Taj-Mahal/Construction-of-the-Taj-Mahal.php.

PART I

1. "Genius," Merriam-Webster, https://www.merriam-webster.com/dictionary/genius.

CHAPTER 1

1. Alex Ambrose, "Her Music: Today's Emerging Female Composer," WQXR, August 20, 2014, https://www.wqxr.org/story/her-music-emerging-female-composer-today/.
2. "Lenny Bernstein and Women Composers: The Bachtrack Classical Music Statistics for 2018," Bachtrack, January 7, 2019, https://bachtrack.com/classical-music-statistics-2018.

CHAPTER 2

1. Nick Anderson, "Appeals Court Upholds Ruling That Harvard Admissions Process Does Not Discriminate Against Asian Americans," *Washington Post*, November 12, 2020, https://www.washingtonpost.com/education/2020/11/12/harvard-admissions-asian-americans-ruling/.
2. Brené Brown, *The Gifts of Imperfection: Let Go of Who You Think You're Supposed to Be and Embrace Who You Are* (Center City, MN: Hazelden, 2010), pp. 87–88.

PART II

1. "Power of the Purse: How Sub-Saharan Africans Contribute to the U.S. Economy," New American Economy, January 2018, http://research.newamericaneconomy.org/wp-content/uploads/sites/2/2018/01/NAE_African_V6.pdf.
2. Stella U. Ogunwole, Karen R. Battle, and Darryl T. Cohen, "Characteristics of Selected Sub-Saharan African and Caribbean Ancestry Groups in the United States: 2008–2012," United States Census Bureau, June 2017, https://www.census.gov/content/dam/Census/library/publications/2017/acs/acs-34.pdf.

CHAPTER 5

1. Jonathan Ringel, "How I Made Partner: Akin Gump's Nnedi Ifudu Nweke," Law.com, March 11, 2019, https://www.law.com/2019/03/11/how-i-made-partner-akin-gumps-nnedi-ifudu-nweke/.

CHAPTER 6

1. The term tiger mother is an expression coined to refer to an exceedingly strict female parent whose overriding concern is that her child does exceptionally well at school. The concept of the tiger mother is most often associated with Asian parents, particularly those of Chinese origin. https://www.macmillandictionary.com/us/buzzword/entries/tiger-mother.html.

PART III

1. John Maxwell, *21 Irrefutable Laws of Leadership* (Thomas Nelson, 1998).
2. Charles Duhigg, *The Power of Habit* (Random House, 2012), p. xvi.

IMMIGRACE JOURNAL BRILLIANCE BLUEPRINT #3

1. Jack Canfield with Janet Switzer, *The Success Principles: How to Get from Where You are to Where You Want to Be* (William Morrow, 2006), pp. 76–78); Gail Matthews, "Goals Research Summary," https://www .dominican.edu/sites/default/files/2020-02/gailmatthews-harvard -goals-researchsummary.pdf.

CHAPTER 12

1. Visit the website here: https://www.thewiesuite.com.

PART V

1. Margaret A. Boden, *The Creative Mind: Myths and Mechanisms* (London: Weidenfeld & Nicolson, 1990; expanded ed., London: Abacus, 1991). For a detailed precis see http://www2.psych.utoronto.ca/users /reingold/courses/ai/cache/bbs.boden.html.
2. Eric Weiner, "The Secret of Immigrant Genius," the *Wall Street Journal*, January 15, 2016, https://www.wsj.com/articles/the-secret-of -immigrant-genius-1452875951.
3. Greg McKeown, "How Play Enriches Our Creative Capacity," fs blog, 2015, https://fs.blog/2015/01/eeesntialism-play-mckeown/.
4. Michelle Martin, "Learning to Trust Your Women's Intuition," Huffington Post, June 7, 2017, https://www.huffpost.com/entry/womens -intuition_b_10192222.

CHAPTER 15

1. Laura Giadorou Koch, "What Is Normal? Are We REALLY Shifting to a More Caring Economy?" *Business Fit Magazine*, November/December 2020, 38–41, https://issuu.com/businessfitmagazine/docs/bfm _nov_dec_2020_screen_mr/38.

Index

About the Author

CHINWE ESIMAI is an award-winning lawyer, trailblazing corporate executive, writer, and speaker who helps women leaders discover and embrace their genius and live lives of impact and fulfillment. Chinwe was born in Nigeria, and along with her mother and her four siblings, she relocated to the United States in 1995.

She is managing director and chief anti-bribery officer at Citigroup, Inc. She is the first person to hold this title in the bank's history. She spent a combined five years at Goldman Sachs in various regulatory risk-management roles. She served as a law professor at the University of St. Thomas School of Law. She began her career as a corporate associate at LeBoeuf, Lamb, Greene & MacRae, LLP.

She has received numerous awards including *American Banker*'s Most Powerful Women in Banking, *Diversity* Magazine's Elite 100 Black Women Changing the Face of Corporate America, Leading Ladies Africa's Most Inspiring Women; *Tropics Magazine*'s Most Powerful Africans Shaping the Future of Africa; Nigerian Lawyers Association Trailblazer of the Year; Face2Face Africa Corporate Leadership Award; and *Ozy* magazine's list of "Angelic Troublemakers," creative thinkers helping to reset America and the world. She is an executive council member of the Ellevate Network and serves as a Cherie Blair Foundation mentor.

Chinwe is the host of the *Brilliance Beyond Borders* podcast. Her leadership insights have also been featured on her blog (chinweesimai .com) and in leading publications around the world, including *Forbes*,

Thrive Global, *Black Enterprise*, Medium, *Real Business UK*, and Knowledge@Wharton. She has delivered keynotes to prestigious audiences around the world and has spoken three times at the United Nations.

She obtained a bachelor of arts in political science, summa cum laude, from the City College of New York and a juris doctor from Harvard Law School. She lives in Sparta, New Jersey, with her husband and three children.

Chinwe loves spending time with her family—her favorite people in the world. In addition to writing, she thoroughly enjoys reading, dancing, exercising, traveling the world, and can often be spotted donning a hat and a smile.